BART'S
FISH
TALES

BART VAN OLPHEN

WITH PHOTOGRAPHY
BY DAVID LOFTUS

BART'S
FISH
TALES

A FISHING ADVENTURE
IN OVER 100 RECIPES

PAVILION

CONTENTS

HELLO LOVELY PEOPLE, JAMIE OLIVER HERE.

It's my total pleasure to introduce you to the one and only Bart van Olphen and his wonderful cookbook, *Bart's Fish Tales*. This book has been an absolute labour of love for Bart, and has taken him to some of the most hard-to-reach places on the planet. I have never seen a fish book where the author has travelled so widely to tell his personal story and those of the sustainable fishing communities he's visited, which is, at the end of the day, what this book is all about. Of course, it's a celebration of how wonderful, healthy and diverse fish can be, but most importantly it's a picture of the humongous pressure that's been put on our oceans as a result of overfishing. Not only will Bart show you how to navigate between the fish that are sustainable and those that are endangered, he will get you asking the right questions of yourself and your fishmonger.

I first learnt about Bart back in 2013 when I spotted his 15-second cooking videos on his Instagram feed @BartsFishTales. It was brilliant, and I immediately started telling people about him. It was his passion and enthusiasm for sharing his incredible knowledge of fish and how to cook it that has made me love his work ever since.

The recipes in this book are inspired by many, many countries around the world, and as delicious and beautiful as his food is, it's also simple and accessible for the everyday cook. You'll find many of them up on his YouTube channel, also called Bart's Fish Tales, and Instagram, which you can use for extra help along the way. I'm sure you'll love the following pages, with pictures captured by the legend, David Loftus, who I've had the pleasure of working with for many years. But for now, on to the book. Enjoy!

Big love,

Jamie O xx

MY PASSION FOR FISH

BART VAN OLPHEN

Where did I get this passion for fish? People often ask me but I don't really know exactly when it started. I can certainly remember as a young boy being fascinated by the huge platters of *fruits de mer* that were brought to the table when we holidayed in Paris each year. Or the time in Belgium when I fell asleep on my mother's lap during lunch. When I awoke and looked up, I saw this incredible monster with huge claws crawling towards me. My father had asked the waiter to bring the lobster and allow it to walk across the table to make sure it was really fresh. What made a very big impression on me was wandering around markets on holiday, and I was particularly taken with the boats moored in the harbour behind the market. And then a little later a fresh fish – fried quickly and served with a slice of lemon – in a noisy local bar. So simple, yet so delicious.

The fisherman's life had long captured my imagination, but it was in the 1990s that I developed a real passion for fish when I had the honour of working in various Michelin-starred restaurants in Paris. I had been dreaming of a French culinary adventure and when the opportunity arose, I soon realised that my preference was for cooking with fish. It was tough working in those traditional Parisian kitchens, but it was during this period that I learned the most as a chef. For me, it was not all about innovative recipes but about classic fish dishes, executed to perfection.

That perfection began with the supplier who arrived each day, usually just after the baker had delivered the bread. He brought freshly caught fish of the finest quality – in the French capital they accepted nothing less – and always a whole fish, which stared back at you with clear eyes and was so fresh it slipped out of your hand. After that came the gutting, filleting and preparation and, in most cases, the latter was as simple as possible. The most important lesson I took back

to Holland with me was that if you want fish at its best, don't do too much to it.

Those are the experiences and memories that inspired me to get involved with fish myself. Back in Amsterdam I opened my own fish shop, which meant finding out more about the story behind fish. I got to know the suppliers and how they worked and became familiar with the industry that provides the fish we eat each day. My romantic vision of small boats and picturesque harbours soon evaporated when I saw the gigantic ships – floating factories that trawled for fish and threw much back into the sea. It was totally profit-driven and the wastage was huge. It was the moment, sometime in 2007, that my search for sustainably caught fish began. A quest for fish with a story.

As you may already know, around 80 per cent of the fish stocks in the world's oceans are being fished to their maximum or beyond. If we continue like this, there will be no fish left to eat by 2048, and that is no exaggeration. In recent decades we have literally plundered the seas and, the careless way we treat the fish we catch makes it worse. Figures show that around 93.4 million tonnes of fish are caught globally each year but that's not the whole total. Over ten million tonnes of fish are thrown overboard for no good reason and many of those are dead by the time they are back in the water. That's an average of 1.5 kg/3 lb 5 oz of fish per person that is wasted globally, which equals ten fish meals a year.

Fish is the last food that we extract *en masse* from the wild so it's vital to realize that we can't harvest more than nature – in this case, the sea – provides. Unlike strawberries, for example, where if there's a shortage we can simply plant more, or organic chickens, where any increase in demand can be met by increasing the birds' living space and the scale of production. These

are things that can be regulated and controlled but it's a different matter with fish. Demand is not equal to supply as that depends entirely on what the sea can offer. We have to understand, and with humility, that we are part of a larger ecological cycle. We can enjoy cooking fish and take pleasure in eating it, but, by the same token, we must ensure that future generations can also continue to eat the finest fish. Sustainability is not about rules but about an intrinsic desire and motivation to do things properly.

Should we eat less fish? Of course not, but we should make conscious choices. In the last ten years much has been done to make consumers aware and to increase the supply of sustainably caught fish. Yet the supply is still sadly limited, certainly in restaurants and fish shops.

I love fish. Preparing fish is what I enjoy doing most and there's nothing I like eating more. There are so many varieties of fish and so many ways to prepare them. Marinated, fried, baked in the oven, deep-fried, poached – many different methods are described in this book. The flavours are diverse and, best of all, you don't need to do very much to create a delicious fish meal.

My aim in this book is to tell the stories behind the fish and to inspire everyone to start cooking with good, well-flavoured fish. It had long been an ambition of mine to work with photographer David Loftus, the simplicity of his work is quite amazing. What you see is what you get and that's not just true of his food photography, it's equally true of his portraits of people. It was fantastic to travel with David and to experience life in sustainable fishing communities together. Catching fish in sustainable ways is about maintaining fish stocks and methods of fishing,

yet even more important is the philosophy of the people involved in fishing. Wherever we were in the world, the way of life was identical. Fishing communities have an awareness of the part they play in the ecological cycle that goes back generations. If they catch too much today, tomorrow they'll be out of work. You can see this lifestyle, this way of living and catching fish, reflected in their faces. David has captured it superbly in his portraits and you have to admit that a fish with a story tastes so much better!

Our trip took us to different fishing communities that are an example to the rest of the world. Each chapter in this book contains recipes featuring fish caught in a particular country. We would draw inspiration from the culinary traditions of a region, but we didn't restrict ourselves to that region alone. After all, you can make a superb classic French *sole à la meunière* with a tonguefish (small sole) from Gambia. The hundred-plus recipes in this book come from all corners of the globe. We have tried to create a balance between different types of fish and shellfish, different cooking methods and dishes for breakfast, lunch or dinner. In this book I want to show that cooking with fish does not need to be very difficult and offers endless variety.

My aim is to show you how to enjoy the best and most delicious fish and, at the same time, I hope to demonstrate that the sea is not in a healthy state, which means that it's vital to start taking action now, together. We should really only eat fish that is sustainably caught as it is the only way to ensure our children and grandchildren will also be able to enjoy the finest and most delicious fish.

AN AMAZING ADVENTURE

DAVID LOFTUS

My obsession with all things oceanic has been passed down the Loftus family tree for generations as far back as the time of Nelson and the Battle of Trafalgar. My Father Eric used to sail an old Thames fishing lighter off the coast of his weekend home in Whitstable in Kent. Growing up in Chelsea, as he did before me, my love of all things nautical, from books to charts, from beachcombing to beach craft, influenced me enough to dwell upon an old Thames Houseboat for fifteen years, much to the chagrin of my loved ones.

The boat, *Candy Coloured Tangerine*, is no longer, but I write this now on my 1921 Dutch-built sailing Tjalk, the *Zwee Gezusters*, moored in Chelsea; how my Father would have loved it, surrounded by the water, and the books of his and my youth, from *The Old Man and The Sea* to *Swallows and Amazons*, from *On the Waterfront* to the ultimate fishermen's novel *Moby Dick*.

Boat-dwelling, beachcombing and an obsession with a nautical past however do not a successful fisherman make! I have tried, with rod, fly and net, and even a tickling technique, but I have not caught more than a few childhood sticklebacks and minnows. Maybe it's the lack of a killer instinct, maybe just bad luck, but so many days have I sat there staring into the murky depths of the Thames, wondering what lurks beneath the surface. I've seen, over the years, cormorants struggling with huge-headed eels the like of which I would never have believed could live beneath Old Father Thames; I've seen grey seals in the centre of London munching on fat silvery fish, I have even seen dolphins, porpoises and a pilot whale, but not a fishy have I caught.

In the last year I have seen more fish than I will probably see in a lifetime. I have travelled the world with Bart, a true gentleman, and a much needed champion for sustainable fishermen and women everywhere. The journey itself has been epic, physically and mentally, and it has been an extraordinary adventure, educationally.

Never again will I take for granted the humble bass or skate, or the sardine or anchovy, even the tiny garnish of a mussel or clam, so easy for us to eat, or even leave on the side of our plate after a long night out, but so very, very, very hard to catch, so tough, so dangerous for the fishermen sent out to feed us. The dangers I have had to face pale into insignificance compared to those faced daily, often nightly, by the men and women I have met on my worldwide Bart-shared escapades.

It doesn't seem to make a lot of short-term financial sense to fish sustainably, but these fishing communities believe in the long-term gains, for themselves, but also for the world's oceans, often putting themselves in extreme danger from unscrupulous and uncaring international fishing fleets. These boats, often fishing illegally, are content to dredge the seas of all their fish, regardless of species or rarity, without a care for the long-term damage, or, as I saw off the coast of Gambia, for human lives. Many a Gambian fisherman has lost his life after being rammed by a fishing boat at night, lights turned off to evade detection. Very sad indeed ... I am so glad and honoured to play my very small part in honouring them.

D X

SUSTAINABLE FISHING

Huge expanses of our oceans are overfished. To ensure that we, and generations to come, can continue to enjoy fish we must make responsible choices. Naturally that applies to fish caught at sea but it also applies to fish bred and farmed in confined spaces. Responsibly farmed fish are identifiable in shops by their ASC label (Aquaculture Stewardship Council).

Catching fish at sea is sustainable if the fishery takes into account the effect their activities are having on the ecosystem in which they operate. In a responsible fishery, there are enough fish left to swim away so they can reproduce in large numbers. So, by all means, catch fish, but always in moderation. A responsible fishing community will always ensure that their fishing causes as little damage to the seabed as possible and minimizes any bycatch. In addition, the fishery should be well organized and managed to ensure that the provenance of each fish can be traced.

Fish from boats that follow these guidelines are often certified and labelled with an MSC blue fish from the Marine Stewardship Council. The MSC is the only independent worldwide certification programme for sustainable fishing that meets the standards set by the United Nations Food and Agriculture Organization (FAO). This is the most reliable way of identifying fish that has been sustainably caught. The MSC programme is founded on a staggering amount of scientific knowledge by which the various fisheries are assessed. Every step of the assessment process is undertaken with the utmost transparency. This means that an MSC-certified fishery can only supply produce bearing an MSC blue fish label on condition that each link in the assessment chain has its own MSC certificate assuring traceability. Although we know that all fish with an MSC label are sustainably caught, it does not necessarily mean that all sustainably caught fish meet the MSC standard. Because we wanted to be one hundred per cent certain, for this book we only used fish with an MSC label. Please consider doing the same.

For wild, traceable, sustainable seafood, look for the blue fish.

www.msc.org

RIF ICELAND

NEWLYN UK

NOVA SCOTIA CANADA

NEW ORLEANS USA

BRUFUT GAMBIA

OUR JOURNEY
AROUND THE WORLD

YERSEKE <u>NETHERLANDS</u>

GETARIA <u>SPAIN</u>

KOLLAM <u>INDIA</u>

MANDHOO <u>MALDIVES</u>

EXMOUTH <u>AUSTRALIA</u>

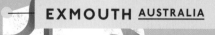

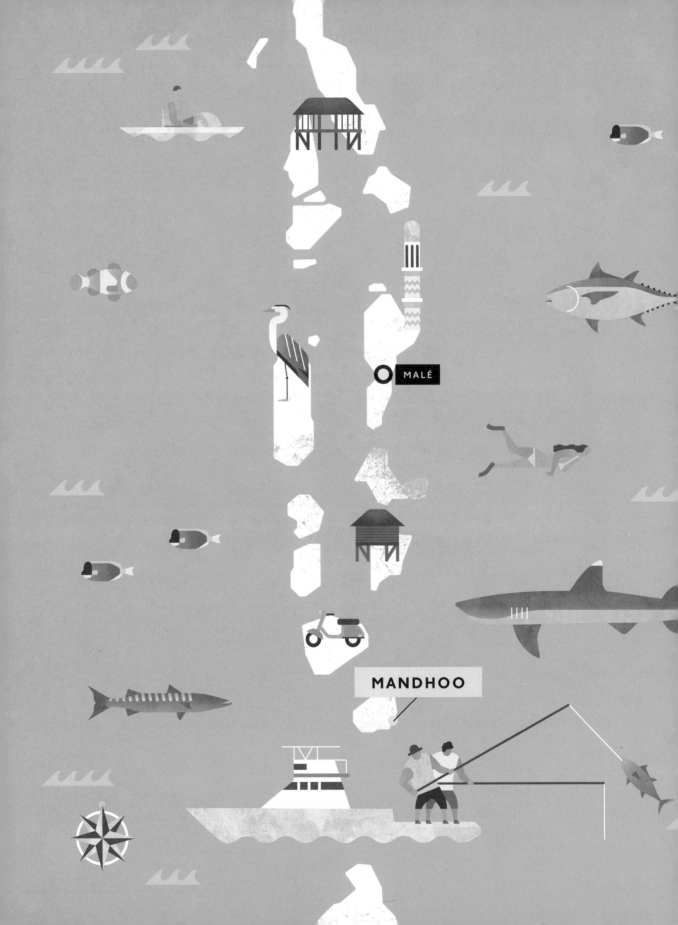

MALÉ

MANDHOO

MALDIVES

TUNA

LAAMU ATOLL, MALDIVES — 1°57'44.6"N 73°25'09.8"E

FAO 51 INDIAN OCEAN W

FISHERMEN — HUSSAIN & AHMED

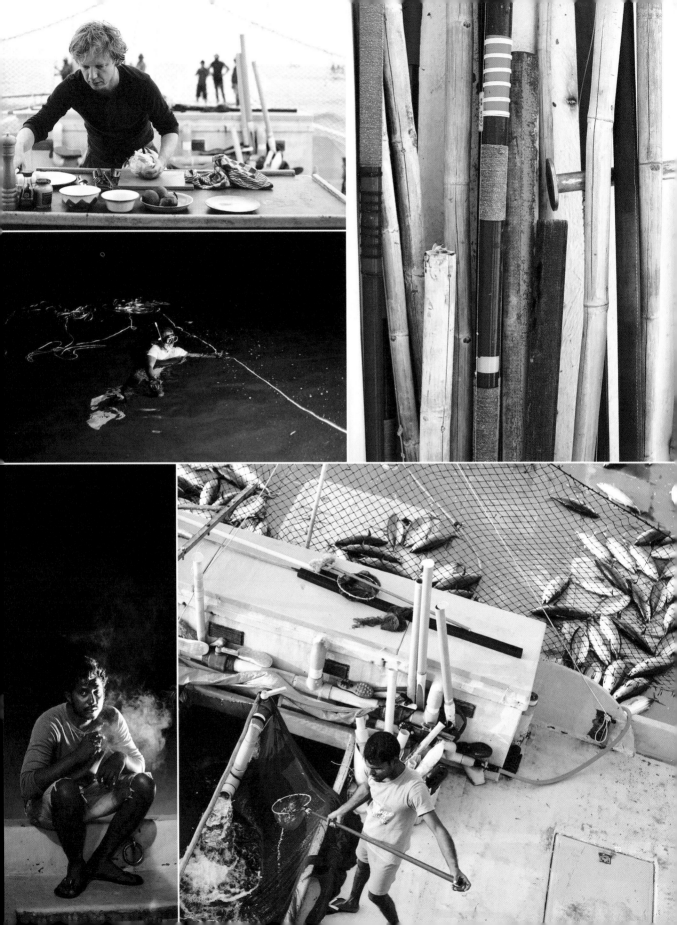

REELED IN
ONE BY ONE

— ⌁ —

Somewhere in the Indian Ocean, close to the equator, a boat bobs up and down on the waves. You can see into the far distance by the light of the moon and stars and no land is in sight. The *dhoni*, a traditional Maldivian fishing boat, has two decks over a cabin but the rest of the boat is flat. The weather is warm and several fishermen are asleep on deck, each one resting on a small pillow.

The tuna fishermen on board need little more than a rod, a pair of shorts and a cushion. Some wear hats and one of them has brought a kind of plastic police helmet, the purpose of which will become clear in the morning. Mandhoo, a small island in the west of the archipelago, has the same white beaches and palm trees boasted by all 'Bounty Islands' and for which the Maldives are so famous. However, there are no luxury resorts, golf courses or honeymooning couples here. On Mandhoo the islanders fish for a living. Steel boxes are stacked high beside the palm trees that line the harbour. The following day the tuna will be delivered in these boxes to the canning factory where the wives of the fishermen work.

Apart from tourism, fishing is the main source of income in the Maldives. Of all the fish caught, over eighty per cent is tuna. Little grows on these tiny islands and rice and other staple foods are delivered from the mainland. Tuna is not just the fishermen's livelihood, it is also their main food source, so tuna is on the menu whether it is breakfast, lunch or dinner. In the afternoon, one of the fishermen on board grates coconut to make *mas-uni*, a fresh tuna salad with shredded coconut and lime, spiced with fiery local chillies (chiles). They eat the salad with flat naan bread and it will be tomorrow's breakfast.

Two types of tuna are caught: skipjack (also known as *bonito* or striped tuna, although the latter name is rarely used) and yellowfin. Skipjack is doing comparatively well as there is plenty in different parts of the ocean. The prospects for yellowfin are less favourable, although the Maldives MSC certificate covers that too, the only place in the world to be accredited apart from a fishery in Mexico. Tuna are caught here in a highly sustainable way, one by one with a pole and line.

Captain Hussein sails out of Mandhoo harbour at around 4pm with twelve men on board. While the fishermen grab a couple of hours sleep during the night, Hussein keeps an eye on the ocean. On one side of the boat two large lamps shine their light into the water so, while the rest of the ocean is pitch black, the spotlights pick out dolphins and huge stingrays shooting under the boat. A couple of hours later, a dark shadow appears, made up of hundreds of tiny fish. The fishermen scoop them out of the water and into a bath filled with seawater.

These are the fish they will use to catch tuna. Once there is sufficient bait the boat picks up speed and heads off to where the tuna swim. Soon the sun comes up and within an hour it is light. Tiny birds appear to be flying around the boat but they are in fact flying fish, some of which can glide a metre or more above the surface. Other *dhonis* appear on the horizon and suddenly the relaxed, tropical mood on-board changes as the fishing begins in earnest.

A net is stretched vertically across the width of the boat and the fishermen form a row at the back. Each has their own rod, just a long, plastic stick with a line and hook on the end. Every couple of minutes, two of the fishermen scatter bait over the side of the *dhoni* to attract the tuna, while Hussein keeps the boat moving at a steady, slow pace. They only fish until the bait is used up so as to ensure they never catch entire shoals and because they use rods, there is virtually no bycatch.

It doesn't take long for the first rod to bend, followed by another. The small, wiry Maldivian fishermen toss the skipjacks over their shoulders with huge strength, and one after another the tuna sail through the air into the upright net. Without looking around, they cast their hooks back into the water, and it becomes clear why one fisherman decided to bring a helmet.

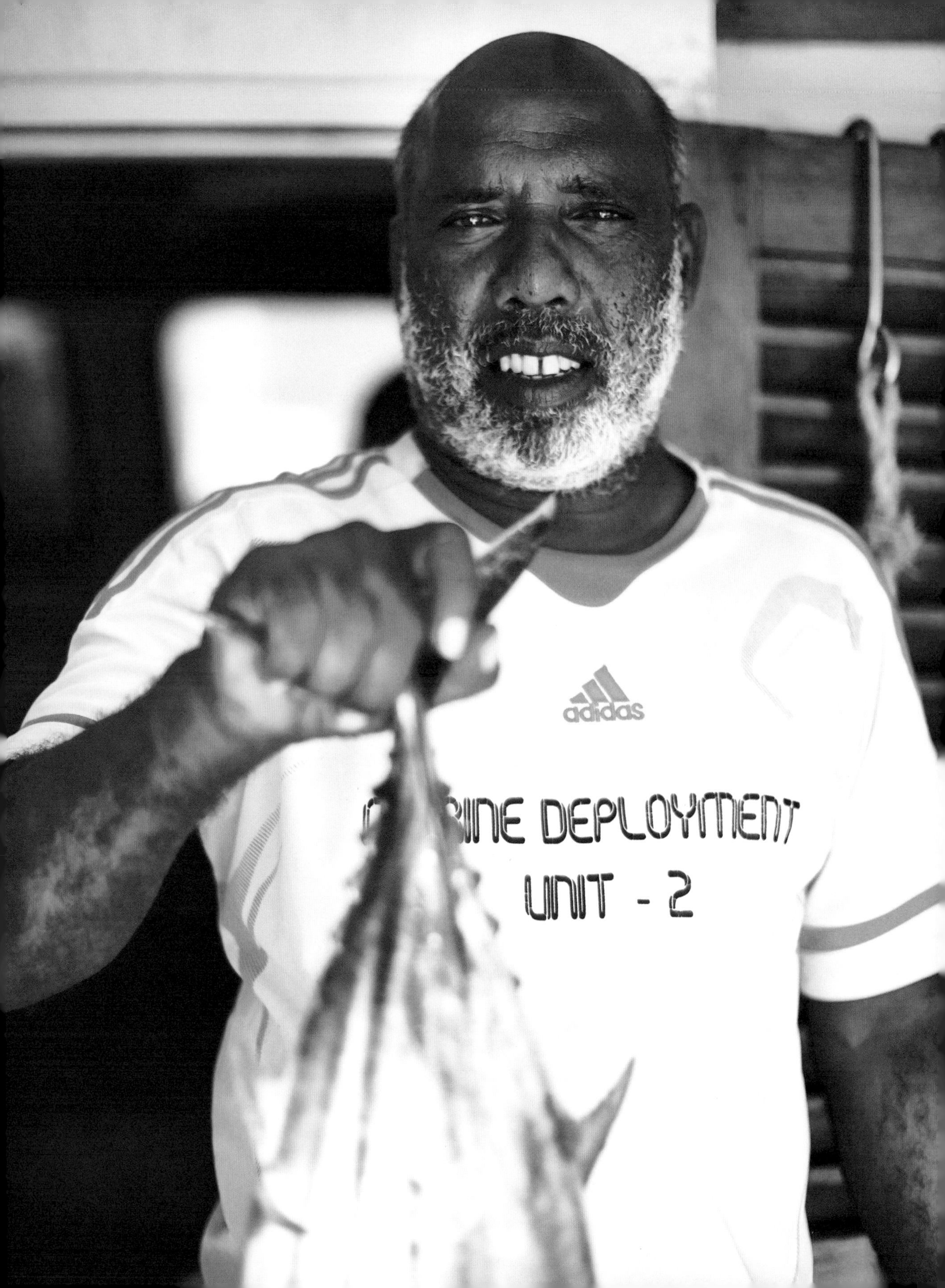
adidas
DEPLOYMENT
UNIT - 2

TUNA 'TARTARE' WITH PONZU SHOYU

STARTER, LUNCH — SERVES 4
PREPARATION 50 MINUTES

This salad takes inspiration from a tuna tartare but to make the best of the meaty fish you chop the flesh more coarsely. Bringing together a tartare requires a combination of flavours and textures. I love Japanese cuisine – it is pure and fresh and ingredients are treated with the utmost resect. Everything tastes better with ponzu. Here it adds delicious flavour without overpowering the delicate tuna. If you prefer a finer dice, you can chop all of the ingredients more finely for a happy tartare.

INGREDIENTS

PONZU SHOYU

100 ml/3 fl oz/generous 1/3 cup
    soy sauce
5 tbsp lemon juice
4 tsp orange juice
2 tbsp dashi, cooled
2 tbsp rice vinegar
2 tbsp mirin

TARTARE

1 tbsp white sesame seeds
200 g/7 oz skipjack or yellowfin
    tuna fillet, cut into 1-cm/1/2-
    inch cubes
1 spring onion (scallion),
    trimmed and finely chopped
1-cm/1/2-inch piece of fresh
    root ginger, peeled and finely
    chopped
2 avocados, peeled, pitted and
    diced
handful of coriander (cilantro)
    leaves
handful of daikon leaves
1/2 cucumber, deseeded and
    coarsely chopped
1/2 red onion, thinly sliced

ALTERNATIVE FISH

albacore tuna*

*There are a few MSC-certified
    yellowfin tuna fisheries in the
    world, such as in the Solomon
    Islands and along the east
    coast of Australia.*

To make the ponzu shoyu dressing, combine the soy sauce, lemon juice, orange juice, dashi, rice vinegar and mirin in a bowl. Set aside for at least 30 minutes to let the flavours develop.

To make the tartare, roast the sesame seeds in a dry frying pan (skillet) until they are golden brown. Remove the seeds from the pan and leave to cool.

In a large bowl, combine the tuna, spring onion (scallion), ginger and avocados with half the sesame seeds, coriander (cilantro) and daikon leaves, reserving the rest. Add the dressing and mix well. Add the cucumber and red onion and mix again with your hands.

Divide between four serving plates and sprinkle with the remaining sesame seeds, coriander and daikon leaves.

'MAS-ROSHI'
MALDIVIAN TUNA SALAD

CANAPÉ, STARTER, LUNCH — SERVES 4
PREPARATION **50 MINUTES** — COOKING **20 MINUTES**

The first time I travelled with food writer Joël Broekaert, who assisted me in writing this book, was when we visited the tuna fishery in the Maldives. The food took some getting used to as it was tuna three times a day – tuna curry, tuna in sauce, tuna in another sauce or fried tuna. The fish was also cooked differently from the way we were used to, making it rather dry and often overdone. However, one dish stood out as truly memorable, a local speciality called mas-uni. Joël was immediately smitten and gorged on this irresistible tuna salad, flavoured with coconut and lime, three times a day, three days in a row. Even at breakfast the mas-uni was spiced with extremely hot local pepper. Joël, of course, reaped what he had sowed and that cold shower was suddenly quite pleasant. When mas-uni is used as a filling for a pasty, the dish is called mas-roshi.

INGREDIENTS

DOUGH

250 g/9 oz/1 ¾ cups plain
   (all-purpose) flour
100 g/4 oz fresh coconut, grated
2 tbsp coconut oil
100 ml/3½ fl oz/generous
   ⅓ cup lukewarm water
salt

TUNA SALAD

2 red onions, chopped
2 red chillies (chiles), deseeded
   and finely chopped
8 fresh (or dried) curry leaves,
   finely chopped
juice of 2 limes
½ tsp salt
90 g/3½ oz fresh coconut,
   grated
2 x 200-g (6-oz /6½-oz) cans of
   skipjack tuna, drained
2 limes, halved

To make the dough, mix the flour, grated coconut, coconut oil and water together in a large bowl. Season with salt and knead to make a smooth dough. Cover and chill in the refrigerator for 30 minutes.

To make the salad, wearing thin plastic gloves to protect your hands from the chillies (chiles), knead together the chopped onions, chillies, curry leaves and lime juice in a bowl and add the salt. In the Maldives, they say that kneading allows the ingredients to 'fuse' together. Gently mix in the coconut and tuna with your hands, until the tuna has a fine texture. The tuna salad (mas-uni) is now ready.

Take a small piece of dough about the size of a golf ball and press it into a flat round about 5 cm/2 inch in diameter. Holding the dough in one hand, spoon some tuna salad into the centre. Fold the dough around the filling to enclose it completely and reshape into a ball. Press down on the little tuna-filled ball until it is flattened and about 1 cm/½ inch thick.

Heat a dry frying pan (skillet) over a medium-high heat. As soon as it is hot, add the tuna parcels to the pan. Fry them for 6-8 minutes on both sides, turning them over every 2 minutes and making sure the dough is cooked through, including around the sides. Depending on the thickness of your parcels, they may need a little longer.

Cut the tuna parcels in half and serve with the lime halves to squeeze over the top.

VITELLO TONNATO

STARTER, LUNCH — SERVES 4
PREPARATION **10 MINUTES** — COOKING **40 MINUTES**

This is perhaps the most delicate carpaccio. The veal, combined with the outstanding flavour of tuna and anchiovies originates from Piedmont in Italy and is my absolute favourite. Serve at room temperature rather than fridge-cold to show of the softness of the veal slices in this twist on a surf 'n' turf.

INGREDIENTS

300 g/10 oz veal escalope
1 x 200-g (6-oz /6½-oz) can of skipjack tuna, drained
2 anchovy fillets canned in olive oil, drained
3 tbsp mayonnaise, plus extra for garnish
1 tsp white balsamic vinegar
handful of flat-leaf parsley
1 tbsp capers, plus extra for garnish
50 g/2 oz rocket (arugula) leaves
vegetable oil, for frying
extra virgin olive oil, for drizzling
salt and pepper

ALTERNATIVE FISH

albacore tuna

Preheat the oven to 90°C/200°F/Gas Mark ¼.

Season the veal escalope with salt and pepper. Heat 2 tablespoons of vegetable oil in an ovenproof frying pan (skillet) over a high heat and sear the veal escalope for 2 minutes on each side. Transfer the pan to the oven and cook the veal for 20–30 minutes. Test the temperature of the meat with a probe: when the core temperature reaches around 57°C/135°F the veal is perfectly cooked. Remove the meat from the oven, let it cool to room temperature and then cut it into very thin slices.

Put the tuna, anchovy fillets, mayonnaise, white balsamic vinegar, parsley and 1 tablespoon of capers in a food processor and blend until smooth. Taste and season with salt and pepper.

To serve, spread a spoonful of tuna mayonnaise on each plate. Arrange the veal slices on top and spoon over more mayonnaise. Garnish with rocket (arugula) leaves and capers and drizzle with extra virgin olive oil.

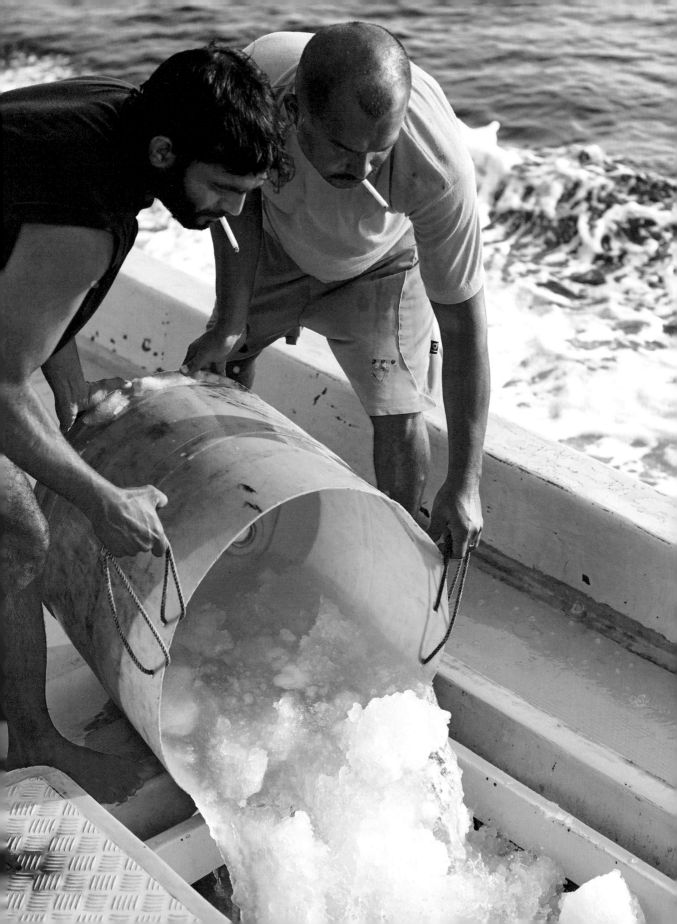

TUNA & MACKEREL ON TOAST

CANAPÉ, LUNCH — SERVES 4
PREPARATION 10 MINUTES — COOKING 5 MINUTES

A good tip to remember when preparing dishes that use canned tuna is to use tuna in oil for dishes that are heated during the preparation so that it won't dry out and use tuna in brine when you intend on adding an oil-based ingredient such as mayonnaise. Always drain your tuna well before use.

INGREDIENTS

1 white baguette
2 x 200-g (6-oz /6½-oz) cans of
  skipjack tuna, drained
8 tbsp mayonnaise
finely grated zest and juice of
  1 lemon
2 tsp capers
½ tbsp finely chopped flat-leaf
  parsley
Little Gem (Bibb) lettuce leaves,
  washed
½ red onion, sliced
¼ Granny Smith apple, cut into
  matchsticks
handful of rocket (arugula)
  leaves
100 g/4 oz mackerel fillet,
  steamed, skinned and broken
  into chunks
1 tbsp finely chopped chives
salt and pepper

ALTERNATIVE FISH

albacore tuna, hot smoked
  salmon

Preheat the grill (broiler).

Cut the baguette into 12 equal-size pieces. Place the pieces cut-side up on a baking sheet and grill (broil) for 3–5 minutes until they are golden brown.

Flake the tuna into a bowl. Mix the mayonnaise with the lemon zest and half the juice. Add half of this lemon mayonnaise to the tuna with the capers and parsley. Season with salt and pepper. Lay the lettuce leaves on two pieces of toast, spoon the tuna mixture on top and add a couple of onion slices.

Spread the rest of the mayonnaise over the remaining pieces of toast. Add a few rocket (arugula) leaves and lay the chunks of mackerel and apple matchsticks on top. Grind over some pepper.

Serve the toasts on a platter or board, garnished with the chives and drizzled with the remaining lemon juice.

TUNA TOASTIE
WITH SAMBAL & ATJAR

BREAKFAST, LUNCH — SERVES 4
PREPARATION 24 HOURS 10 MINUTES — COOKING 5 MINUTES

Tabac is one of the nicest cafés in Amsterdam situated in the nicest spot along the Prinsengracht canal and they serve a tuna toastie with sambal and adjar. I often sit there to have coffee and consider what recipes I will try out next.

INGREDIENTS

300 ml/10 fl oz/1¼ cups white wine vinegar
4 tbsp sugar
1 cucumber, deseeded and cut into long, thin slices
1 onion, thinly sliced
4 spring onions (scallions), topped and tailed
2 x 200-g (6-oz /6½-oz) cans of skipjack tuna, drained
1 red onion, chopped
4 tsp sambal oelek, plus extra to serve
handful of coriander (cilantro) leaves, finely chopped
1 tbsp olive oil
8 slices of white bread
200 g/7 oz Cheddar cheese, grated
oil or melted butter for toasting or frying
salt

ALTERNATIVE FISH

albacore tuna

Heat the vinegar and sugar in a saucepan, stirring until the sugar has dissolved. Leave to cool. Put the cucumber and onion in a jar and pour over the vinegar and sugar so the vegetables are covered. Leave for at least 1 hour, but preferably 24 hours, or longer.

Cut the spring onions (scallions) in half lengthwise and then across into thin slices. Put the tuna, spring onions, red onion, sambal oelek, coriander (cilantro), olive oil and a pinch of salt in a bowl and mix well. Divide the tuna salad between four slices of bread and top with the grated cheese. Cover with the remaining slices of bread.

Brush a sandwich maker with oil or melted butter or heat oil or butter in a frying pan (skillet). Cook the toasties in the sandwich maker, or fry for 2-3 minutes on each side until golden brown.

Serve the toasties with the cucumber and onion pickle and some extra sambal oelek.

GRILLED TUNA WITH SESAME & SOY MAYONNAISE

LUNCH, CANAPÉ, STARTER — SERVES 4
PREPARATION 15 MINUTES — COOKING 2 MINUTES

There are more than twenty types of tuna, or fish that are called tuna, and they all differ in shape and flavour. In fact, distinguishing between them is useful for more than just culinary reasons. It is vital to know which tuna you are buying because some types are more endangered than others. For example, Atlantic bluefin is on the critical list, although other bluefin populations elsewhere in the world are also seriously threatened, so you should definitely not be eating that variety of tuna. The other three types that are commonly eaten are yellowfin, albacore and skipjack. It's confusing that the Latin name for yellowfin is Thunnus albacares, while albacore is Thunnus alalunga. It's far easier to tell which is which when you see them: the flesh of yellowfin is deep red whereas albacore is much paler. Their situation is not as dire as that of bluefin tuna but their numbers are not ideal either. Skipjack, the smallest of these, is in a healthier position. This fish is also known (incorrectly) as bonito, but the real bonito is a close relative of tuna and both are ideal for canning. If you want to grill (broil) tuna, then yellowfin and albacore are more suitable. Always buy tuna that carries an MSC label and preferably one caught with a hook and line. Currently, there is no other fish to which this applies with so much urgency.

INGREDIENTS

4 tbsp mayonnaise
1 tbsp soy sauce
juice of ½ lime
50 g/2 oz/⅓ cup black sesame seeds
50 g/2 oz/⅓ cup white sesame seeds
400 g/14 oz yellowfin tuna fillet, cut into oblong steaks, 4–5 cm/1½–2 inches thick
16 green shiso leaves (optional)
handful of purple shiso leaves
handful of daikon leaves
togarashi (Japanese spice mix)
sunflower oil, for brushing

ALTERNATIVE FISH

albacore tuna

Stir together the mayonnaise, soy sauce and lime juice to make quite a thin sauce.

Spread out the black and white sesame seeds on a flat plate and mix them with your fingers. Brush the tuna steaks lightly on all sides with sunflower oil. Roll the steaks in the sesame seeds, pressing the seeds on gently and making sure they are 'stuck' to the tuna in an even coating.

Have a bowl of cold water and ice cubes ready.

Place a dry frying pan (skillet) over a high heat. As soon as it is hot, add the tuna and sear the steaks for 15 seconds on each side.

Once seared, remove the tuna from the pan and place the steaks in a small plastic freezer bag. Holding the bag closed so no water gets into it, dip the bag in the iced water for 1 minute to prevent further cooking.

Cut the tuna into thin, equal-size slices, 1 cm/⅓ inch thick. If using green shiso leaves, serve the tuna slices on the leaves. Drizzle over some of the mayonnaise and garnish with purple shiso and daikon leaves. Finally sprinkle over a little togarashi.

JAPANESE TUNA BURGER

LUNCH, MAIN COURSE – SERVES 4
PREPARATION 15 MINUTES – COOKING 15 MINUTES

Seafood burgers are simple to make and a great joy to serve. They look amazing! In this recipe I use tuna with teriyaki but you can make it with any species of fish or leftover seafood and marinade that you like. You should add the teriyaki at the latest possible stage because of the sugar content, which will caramelize quickly and may overpower the fish if cooked for too long.

INGREDIENTS

500 g/1 lb 2 oz albacore tuna fillet
1 egg, beaten
6 tbsp panko (or dry) breadcrumbs, plus extra if needed
2 spring onions (scallions), trimmed and finely chopped
2 shallots, chopped
1 tsp togarashi (Japanese spice mix)
4 tbsp mayonnaise
finely grated zest and juice of 1 lime
1 avocado
1 tbsp sesame seeds
4 tiger buns (or other burger buns)
5 tbsp teriyaki sauce (see page 341)
100 g/4 oz shiitake mushrooms, sliced
8 iceberg lettuce leaves
60 g/2¼ oz Japanese seaweed salad (chuka wakame)
4 radishes, sliced
groundnut (peanut) oil, for frying
salt

ALTERNATIVE FISH

skipjack or yellowfin tuna

Cut the tuna fillet into small pieces. The finer you cut the pieces, the finer the texture of the burgers will be.

In a large bowl, combine the tuna, egg, panko, spring onions (scallions) and shallots. Season with togarashi and salt. If the mixture still has a 'wettish' feel, mix in some extra panko. Using your hands, shape the tuna mixture into four even-size round burgers.

Mix the mayonnaise with the lime zest and half the juice and set aside. Cut the avocado in half and remove the stone (pit). Scoop out the flesh and cut it into thin slices. Drizzle with the remaining lime juice to prevent discolouration. Toast the sesame seeds in a dry frying pan (skillet) over a medium-high heat for 1–2 minutes until they are well browned. Remove the seeds from the pan and set aside.

Split the buns in half and toast the cut sides on a hot grill pan (broiler pan) until they are a rich golden brown. Stay close as the buns will turn brown very quickly.

Remove the buns, turn up the heat under the grill pan to high and add the tuna burgers. Depending on how thick they are, flip the burgers over after 2–3 minutes. Spread the tops of the burgers with 2 tablespoons of the teriyaki sauce. After 2–3 minutes turn them over again and spread with 2 more tablespoons of the sauce. After 30 seconds flip the burgers over once more to sear the other side briefly. Remove the burgers from the grill and cover with a sheet of foil to keep them warm.

Fry the shiitake mushrooms in 1 tablespoon of groundnut (peanut) oil over a high heat. When they begin to brown – after about 2–3 minutes – add the final tablespoon of teriyaki sauce and mix well. Cook for 30 seconds and then remove from the heat.

To assemble your burgers, spread the bottom halves of the buns with lime mayonnaise. Top each with two lettuce leaves and some seaweed salad. Add the burgers and mushrooms, sprinkle with sesame seeds and lay the avocado and radish slices on top. Spread lime mayonnaise over the cut sides of the bun lids and place on top.

SALADE NIÇOISE

LUNCH, MAIN COURSE — SERVES 4
PREPARATION 10 MINUTES — COOKING 35 MINUTES

I have to admit I only discovered Julia Child around ten years ago when Inge Tichelaar (the stylist for this book) gave me a copy of *Mastering the Art of French Cooking* for my birthday. This epic tome is the definitive work on French cuisine and contains truly inspirational recipes. Julia did a lot of black-and-white television and I started watching her old shows. It made me realise that however beautifully a dish is presented, food always looks less appetizing in black and white. Julia's strength lay in her personality, an elegant woman revisiting so vividly all the things she had encountered on her travels in France. In one programme on salade Niçoise, she arranged the ingredients separately on a large platter — something we'd call 'deconstructed' today — but Julia probably just thought it was a pity to mix everything together as each ingredient looked so beautiful in its own right.

INGREDIENTS
DRESSING
1 tsp Dijon mustard
2 tbsp white wine vinegar
1 garlic clove, finely chopped
3 tbsp sunflower oil
3 tbsp extra virgin olive oil
1 tbsp finely chopped flat-leaf
   parsley
salt

SALAD
300 g/10 oz baby new potatoes,
   halved
150 g/5 oz haricots verts,
   topped and tailed
2 eggs
400 g/14 oz albacore tuna fillet,
   cut into 1–2 cm/
   $^1/_3$–$^3/_4$ inch thick slices
1 small cos (romaine) lettuce
200 g/7 oz tomatoes, halved
2 tbsp black olives, pitted
1 x 50-g (2-oz) can of anchovy
   fillets in olive oil, drained
groundnut (peanut) oil for
   grilling (broiling)
salt and pepper

ALTERNATIVE FISH
yellowfin tuna

To make the dressing, put all the ingredients in a jar, seal tightly with a lid and shake well.

To make the salad, put the potatoes in a pan of cold, lightly salted water, bring to the boil and cook until tender, about 10–15 minutes. Drain and leave the potatoes to cool slightly, but the salad is best if it is served before the potatoes have cooled completely.

Bring another pan of salted water to the boil and cook the beans for 4–5 minutes until they are al dente. Lift out the beans with a slotted spoon and cool them in a bowl of cold water. Boil the eggs in the pan in the same water for 6 minutes, so the yolks are still slightly 'runny'. Drain and plunge the eggs into cold water before peeling and cutting into quarters.

Pat the tuna dry on both sides with kitchen paper (paper towels), brush the fish with groundnut (peanut) oil and sprinkle with salt. Heat a grill pan (broiler pan) over a high heat and, when it is very hot, add the tuna. Grill (broil) for about 1½ minutes on each side, avoiding moving the fillets around in the pan. To mark the tuna with a striking criss-cross pattern, give one side a quarter turn half way through cooking. Remove the tuna from the pan and cover with a piece of foil to keep warm.

Put the new potatoes in a bowl. Remove the leaves from the lettuce and rinse. Add the tomatoes, lettuce leaves and haricots verts to the bowl. Pour over two-thirds of the dressing and toss well. Transfer the mixture to a large serving dish and scatter the olives and anchovies on top. Cut the tuna into pieces and arrange over the salad with the eggs quarters. Season with ground pepper.

Serve with the remaining dressing and some good country bread.

GRILLED FISH SKEWERS
WITH HERB DRESSING

MAIN COURSE — SERVES 4
PREPARATION 20 MINUTES — COOKING 35 MINUTES

To grill (broil) fish on a skewer you should choose a species with a firm, meaty texture, such as swordfish, tuna or salmon. Anything too flaky will just fall apart.

INGREDIENTS

POTATOES & SKEWERS

4 large potatoes in their jackets
100 ml/3 fl oz/generous ⅓ cup crème fraîche (sour cream)
juice of 1 lemon
4 chives, finely chopped
250 g/9 oz yellowfin tuna fillet, cut into 2–3-cm/1¼-inch cubes
250 g/9 oz swordfish fillet, cut into 2–3-cm/1¼-inch cubes
3 red (bell) peppers
1 green (bell) pepper
1 yellow (bell) pepper
1 aubergine (eggplant), sliced
1 courgette (zucchini), sliced
1 lemon, cut into wedges, to serve
a few thyme sprigs, to serve
extra virgin olive oil

HERB DRESSING

1 garlic clove, finely chopped
1 tsp mustard
1 tbsp capers, finely chopped
150 ml/5 fl oz/⅔ cup extra virgin olive oil, plus extra if needed
handful of flat-leaf parsley, finely chopped
handful of basil leaves, finely chopped
1 tbsp red wine vinegar
a few drops of lemon juice
sugar (optional)
salt and pepper

ALTERNATIVE FISH

albacore tuna

For the potatoes, light a barbecue and leave until the coals turn white. Place each potato in the centre of a sheet of foil and drizzle with a few drops of olive oil before wrapping up tightly. Place the potatoes in the barbecue coals and leave until tender when pierced with a skewer.

In a bowl, mix the crème fraîche (sour cream) with the lemon juice and chives. Season with salt and pepper and set aside.

To prepare the skewers, in another bowl, mix the cubed fish with 3 tablespoons of olive oil and season with salt and pepper. Cut one red (bell) pepper and the green and yellow peppers in half, deseed them and cut into small squares, similar in size to the fish cubes. Add the peppers to the bowl of fish and leave to marinate in the oil.

Cut the remaining two red peppers into quarters and remove the seeds. Place skin-side down on the barbecue and grill until the skins are charred. Wrap in foil and leave to cool.

Season the aubergine (eggplant) and courgette (zucchini) slices with salt and pepper. Grill on the barbecue until scorch lines appear, turning the slices over once. Remove from the barbecue and let cool. Pull the skin off the red peppers and cut into strips. Put all the vegetables in a bowl, spoon over some olive oil and season again.

To make the herb dressing, mix the garlic, mustard and capers together. Add the olive oil and mix again. Add the parsley, basil, red wine vinegar and lemon juice. Mix and season with salt and pepper. You can add extra olive oil for a creamier texture, or sugar to cut sourness.

Thread the peppers and fish cubes onto skewers, starting with a square of pepper. followed by a cube of fish, then pepper, fish, and so on. Trim off any protruding pieces of pepper that might burn. Grill the skewers for 1–2 minutes on each side until the fish and peppers are nicely browned but remain soft and succulent inside.

Remove the skewers from the barbecue and place on a platter. Drizzle some dressing over and serve the rest on the side. Lift the potatoes from the hot coals and let cool a little before removing the foil and cutting them open. Top with the chive cream and serve with the skewers, garnished with thyme sprigs and lemon wedges on the side.

FISH SOUP WITH TUNA & PLAICE

LUNCH, STARTER — SERVES 4
COOKING **30 MINUTES**

I love seafood soup, there are so many recipes from around the world to try. The reason being that in the old days you would use the whole of the fish to save waste. The best flavour comes from the head and bones of the fish. Both should be used to make stocks and soups but you can use store-bought stock if you don't have time to prepare the fish stock for this soup.

INGREDIENTS

2 red (bell) peppers, deseeded and cut into small pieces
2 red chillies (chiles), deseeded and finely chopped
8 garlic cloves, finely chopped
2 bay leaves
4 potatoes, peeled and roughly diced
200 ml/7 fl oz/scant 1 cup white wine
750 ml/1 ¼ pints/3 cups fish stock (see page 390)
8 saffron threads
½ tsp paprika
200 g/7 oz albacore tuna fillet, cut into chunks
200 g/7 oz plaice fillet, skinned and cut into chunks
handful of flat-leaf parsley, finely chopped
olive oil and groundnut (peanut) oil, for frying
salt and pepper

ALTERNATIVE FISH

flounder, sole or lemon sole

Heat 4 tablespoons of olive oil in a deep saucepan over a medium heat. Add the red (bell) peppers, chillies (chiles), garlic and bay leaves and fry gently for 10 minutes, stirring frequently. Add the potatoes, wine, stock, saffron and paprika. Season with salt and pepper.

Lower the heat as soon as the soup begins to boil. Cover the pan with a lid and leave to simmer for 10 minutes.

Heat some groundnut (peanut) oil in a frying pan (skillet) and fry the tuna chunks on both sides over a medium heat for 2–3 minutes until they are browned. Remove from the pan and set aside.

Test the potatoes with the tip of a sharp knife – they are almost ready when you feel some resistance as you push the knife in. Add the plaice and half the parsley, cook for 3 minutes, adding the tuna chunks in the final minute. Serve the soup sprinkled with the remaining parsley and accompanied by good country bread.

OTTAWA ⃝

NOVA SCOTIA

CANADA

LOBSTER, CRAB & SCALLOPS

NOVA SCOTIA, CANADA — 46°47'49.6"N 60°16'30.9"W

FAO 21 ATLANTIC OCEAN NW

FISHERMEN — KERRY & RONALD

LOBSTER: THE NATION'S PRIDE

Winters are long in Canada. In Nova Scotia, snow tyres with steel studs are still fitted to vehicles in April because of the amount of ice and snow on the roads. By the time people are ready to change their tyres, the drift ice in St Lawrence Bay is starting to float out to sea. It's the signal that the lobster fishery can open for business, but crab fishermen have to wait a little longer. As crab is fished further out to sea, the drift ice has to have moved well out into open water. Lobster and crab traps are sometimes weighed down by concrete to ensure they stay on the bottom, but if the buoy to which they are attached gets caught on an ice floe and drifts away, it is lost forever.

While spider (snow) crab may be tastier, Nova Scotia is more famous for its lobster. Canadian lobsters are sold around the world but most of the lobsters caught around the Nova Scotia peninsula go to the Canadian east coast. The people are proud of this and advertise their lobsters on hoardings along the roads. From the smartest restaurant to the simplest café, lobster is always on the menu. Even McDonald's here sells lobster rolls – a bread roll filled with lobster salad – and the international airport at Halifax offers a special packing service, allowing passengers to take live lobsters as baggage. According to the Guinness Book of Records, the biggest lobster ever found – a giant weighing over 20 kg/44 lb – was caught off Nova Scotia.

Thanks to the cooperatives, the fishing industry is largely owned by the people who actually do the fishing, so the money they earn remains in the local economy. Despite this, the fishing villages are still in trouble because the sons and daughters of fishing families are moving away to live elsewhere. Lobster fishing is hard work and there are few alternatives in Nova Scotia. The landscape is spectacular but the peninsula is sparsely populated and distances are huge.

However, fishing is a lot less arduous than it used to be, as Ronald Ingram, the oldest fisherman in the village, recalls. The lobster traps look pretty much the same as they did in his day – wire mesh crates with wooden slats and a funnel on either side. They sit on the seabed, tied to a long rope attached to a coloured buoy so they can be easily located. When Ingram started catching lobster back in the 1920s, the fishermen would go out in wooden rowing boats and the traps, weighed down with stones, were hauled in by hand. Working from a boat like that, he recalls they caught around 150 a day, before rowing back as fast as possible to be the first to sell their catch on shore.

Ronald Ingram turns ninety-five next year and while he no longer fishes, he is still working. When the funnel in a lobster trap breaks, it's Ronald who is asked to mend the net. All he needs is an old-fashioned board with a hook attached, which he wedges under his foot. Very few people in the fishing community still have the skill to do this.

Today, the lobster boats have a lot more equipment on board. Skipper Kerry Gracie lays around 250 traps. Every day, six days a week, he hauls them up one by one with his crew of two. A mechanical winch does the heavy work and Kerry logs where he drops the traps overboard on his computer. He has equipment to measure the depth and temperature of the water, the ideal temperature being 4.5°C/40°F, as that's when the lobsters are most active and travel the greatest distances.

Once the lobsters start to moult by shedding their shells, the season is over, but until then Kerry catches as many as he can. There are a few rules to ensure the lobster population remains healthy. For example, there is a minimum size, and lobsters that are too small are thrown back, as are females with eggs under their tail. If a lobster is damaged and therefore cannot be sold, its tail is clipped and it must be thrown back and left until the clip is no longer visible. It takes about three years, but it will have been able to reproduce during that time.

One day back in 1920, one of the crew who used to sail with Ronald Ingram's father was too drunk to go fishing so ten-year-old Ronnie had to take his place and he's been a fisherman ever since. That's how it was in those days and today skipper Kerry takes a youngster along at the weekends, too. Logan is sixteen and still at school, so he comes out at the weekend to help, ensuring that the skills of the Nova Scotia lobster fishermen are passed on to the next generation.

RISOTTO WITH LOBSTER

STARTER — SERVES 4

PREPARATION **1 HOUR 25 MINUTES** — COOKING **35 MINUTES**

Lobster is delicious, with bright white flesh that is soft and sweet. However, lobster meat deteriorates quickly as it contains enzymes that start to break down as soon as the creature dies. To keep the meat fresh for as long as possible, the lobster must either be cooked immediately after it has been caught, or kept alive. It's why you often see a tank – or, more accurately, an homarium – containing live lobsters in some restaurants. You choose the one you'd like and the chef prepares and cooks it just before serving. Sadly, though, a live lobster isn't always fresh! A lobster can survive for a long time in a tank, even without food, but eventually it will start to eat its own flesh. It becomes thin and weak and, when cooked, the meat has a mushy texture. You have no way of knowing how long a lobster has been in an homarium, or how long it was before it was put in there. Some merchants keep lobsters for months waiting for prices to rise at the end of the season. Always choose a lively, active lobster as it's the best indication of freshness.

INGREDIENTS

2 x 400–500-g/14 oz–1 lb 2-oz
  live lobsters
2 litres/3½ pints/8½ cups court
  bouillon (see page 392), or
  enough to cover the lobsters,
  or salted water
1 shallot, chopped
300 g/10 oz/1½ cups risotto rice
3 tbsp white wine
1.2 litres/2 pints/5 cups hot
  shellfish bouillon (see page
  390)
25 g/1 oz/2 tbsp butter
1 tbsp finely chopped flat-leaf
  parsley
olive oil
salt and pepper

ALTERNATIVE SHELLFISH

crab or prawns (shrimp)

First render the lobsters unconscious by freezing them for 1 hour. Remove the lobsters from the freezer and leave them for 15 minutes to come to room temperature. Bring the court bouillon or salted water to the boil in a large pan, add the lobsters and boil for 8 minutes. Drain and lightly rinse them under cold running water. Break off the tails and remove the meat. Crack the claws and dig out the meat with a lobster pick (see page 403). Cut all the meat into large chunks and set aside.

Meanwhile, heat 2 tablespoons of olive oil in a deep frying pan (skillet) over a low heat and sauté the shallot for 2 minutes until softened. Add the rice and stir for 2 minutes until the grains are translucent. Deglaze with the white wine and then add 200 ml/ 7 fl oz/scant 1 cup of the shellfish bouillon. When the rice has absorbed almost all the liquid, add more bouillon, stirring constantly. Continue to add the bouillon in the same way until the rice is cooked but still has a little 'bite'. This will take about 20 minutes.

Stir in the butter, the lobster meat and the parsley and season with salt and pepper.

CRAB LEGS
IN TARRAGON BUTTER

CANAPÉ, STARTER, LUNCH — SERVES 4
COOKING 15 MINUTES

Why does fish go so well with tarragon? Fennel, tarragon, Pernod, anything with the aniseed flavour pairs wonderfully well with seafood. It is fragrant enough that you don't really need to add much else except for a cold glass of crisp white wine. Herbs often dictate the flavour of a dish, although parsley, by far the most widely used herb and an excellent one to use, does not dominate particularly. It's hard to spoil a recipe by adding too much of it. Most people like basil, which doesn't have a particularly strong flavour, but leaf coriander (cilantro) is a different matter entirely. Some people think it's the best herb on the planet, while others think it tastes like soap. It can ruin an entire dish if you're not a fan. Tarragon has a pronounced aniseed taste that you have to like. Of all the aniseed-flavoured herbs and spices, such as fennel and star anise, I think tarragon is the best. In this recipe, the crab and the tarragon are equally important flavours and together they make the dish. You really don't need much else.

INGREDIENTS

700 g/1 lb 8 oz crab legs,
    cooked or raw
40 g/1 1/2 oz/3 tbsp butter
handful of tarragon leaves,
    coarsely chopped
handful of flat-leaf parsley,
    coarsely chopped
1/2 lemon
salt and pepper

If you use raw crab legs, cook them for 6–8 minutes in boiling, salted water and then drain and leave to cool.

Split the crab legs lengthwise and open them to expose the meat.

Heat 75 g/3 oz/6 tbsp of the butter in a frying pan (skillet) over a medium heat. As soon as the butter starts to sizzle, add the crab legs and fry for 2–3 minutes, shaking the pan occasionally. Add the tarragon and, after 1 minute, the parsley and the rest of the butter. Season with salt and pepper and squeeze the juice from the half lemon into the pan. Fry for a further 1 minute.

Serve the crab legs with the tarragon butter sauce spooned over.

OMELETTE WITH LOBSTER & CHIVES

BREAKFAST, STARTER, LUNCH — SERVES 4
PREPARATION 1 HOUR 30 MINUTES — COOKING 15 MINUTES

While we were travelling in Canada, I asked David Loftus – who took the fantastic photograhs for this book – to name his favourite fish dish. 'Omelette with lobster', he said. It's a really simple dish if well made and extremely tasty if the best ingredients are used. It also seemed a particularly apt choice as it's just how David takes his photographs. He uses natural light without flash and doesn't try to enhance the appearance of things. Even working within these constraints, he still manages to take the best photos in the world. The next morning I decided to surprise him so, as the sun was rising, I cooked David a lobster omelette on a barbecue in the snow outside his hotel window. Unfortunately he never got to taste it. He was momentarily distracted by the glorious sight of the sun rising over the ice and at that exact moment the hotel dog snatched the omelette and ran off with it. I need to make one for David again soon.

INGREDIENTS

500–600-g/1 lb 2-oz–1 lb 5-oz live lobster or 200 g/7 oz cooked lobster meat
2 litres/3½ pints/8½ cups court bouillon (see page 392), or enough to cover the lobster, or salted water
8 slices of bread
12 eggs
2 tbsp cream or milk (optional)
handful of chives, finely chopped
groundnut (peanut) oil
salt and pepper

ALTERNATIVE FISH

crab or prawns (shrimp)

If using a live lobster, render it unconscious by placing it in the freezer for 1 hour. Remove and leave it for 15 minutes to come to room temperature. Bring the court bouillon or salted water to the boil in a large pan and cook the lobster for 8 minutes. Rinse lightly under cold running water. Break off the tail and remove the meat. Crack the claws and dig out the meat with a lobster pick (see page 403). Cut all the meat into large chunks, divide into four portions and set aside.

Toast the bread in a toaster on medium heat.

To make the first omelette, crack three eggs into a bowl and beat with a whisk. If you prefer, beat all twelve eggs together and divide them when you start to fry. Add the milk or cream, if using, and season with salt and pepper.

Heat 1 tablespoon of groundnut (peanut) oil in a frying pan (skillet) over a high heat and pour in the three beaten eggs. After 30 seconds turn the heat down and cover the pan. As soon as the eggs are set on the bottom, shake the pan gently back and forth to release them from the pan as this will make serving easier. When the surface of the omelette is not quite set, top with one portion of the lobster meat and one-quarter of the chives. Cover the pan again and cook for a further 1 minute. Grind over a little pepper, remove the omelette from the pan and cook three more omelettes in the same way.

Serve the omelettes with the toast.

GRILLED LOBSTER WITH PERNOD & PARSLEY

STARTER, LUNCH — SERVES 4
PREPARATION 1 HOUR 25 MINUTES — COOKING 15 MINUTES

Lobsters and other shellfish are especially prized for their sweet flavour. This sweetness comes from the high proportion of sugar and sweet amino acid in their flesh. The lobster's tail contains the most meat and it is easy to lift this out when eating a grilled half-lobster. Extracting the flesh from the claws is more difficult but the flavour is richer as the lobster makes the muscles in its claws work harder. When you cut a lobster in half you'll see its two claws are not identical. Look carefully and you'll notice one claw is long, thin and sharp – the lobster uses this to cut and tear – while the other is thick and blunt – for squeezing and cracking. This thicker claw has far more meat so if you share lobster on a first date you know who should get the bigger claw.

INGREDIENTS

2 x 500–600-g/1 lb 2-oz–1 lb 5-oz live lobsters
2 litres/3½ pints/8½ cups court bouillon (see page 392), or enough to cover the lobster, or salted walter
100 g/4 oz/8 tbsp butter
1 shallot, roughly chopped
2 garlic cloves, roughly chopped
1 tbsp Pernod
handful of flat-leaf parsley, roughly chopped
salt and pepper

Preheat the grill (broiler).

Put the lobsters in the freezer for 1 hour to render them unconscious. Remove from the freezer and leave for 15 minutes to come to room temperature. Bring the court bouillon or salted water to the boil in a large pan, add the lobsters and boil for 8 minutes. Drain and lightly rinse them under cold running water. Twist off the claws and cut the lobsters in half lengthwise. Cut off the tails and remove the meat. Do the same with the legs (see page 403). Remove the cloudy mass from the heads and set aside. Fill the space in the heads with the meat from the claws and legs, pressing it down firmly.

Blitz the butter, shallot, garlic, Pernod, parsley and the mass from the lobster heads in a food processor, or use a hand blender, mixing thoroughly. Season with salt and pepper. Divide the butter mixture between the lobster halves and lay them, butter-side up, in a grill pan or flameproof dish. Grill (broil) the lobsters for 3–5 minutes or until the topping is golden brown.

LOBSTER WITH PASSION FRUIT & MUSTARD

STARTER, MAIN COURSE — SERVES 4
PREPARATION **1 HOUR 20 MINUTES** — COOKING **20 MINUTES**

My brother Vincent lives in a little fishing town called Tofo in Mozambique. And on the Playa de Tofo (the beach), fishermen bring lobster to sell straight from the boats. Seafood is offered to you but never asked for – you never know what they are going to bring in from their haul so you must cook whatever arrives. I was surprised when I saw Vincent preparing a sauce to dress the lobster using passionfruit with mustard, which binds the sauce, and a squeeze of fresh lime but it is so fresh and zingy that I had to include it in the book.

INGREDIENTS

4 x 500–600-g/1 lb 2-oz–1 lb 5-oz live lobsters (use 2 lobsters for a starter)
2 litres/3½ pints/8½ cups court bouillon (see page 392), or enough to cover the lobsters, or salted water
40 g/1½ oz/3 tbsp butter
2 shallots, chopped
4 passion fruit
2 tsp Dijon mustard
finely grated zest and juice of ½ lime
4 tbsp double (heavy) cream
handful of coriander (cilantro) leaves, chopped
salt and pepper

Put the lobsters in the freezer for 1 hour to render them unconscious. Remove from the freezer and leave for 15 minutes to come to room temperature. Bring the court bouillon or salted water to the boil in a large pan, add the lobsters and boil for 8 minutes. Drain and lightly rinse them under cold running water. You can either remove the lobster meat from the shells now or let your guests do it at the table (see page 403).

Heat the butter in a frying pan (skillet) and fry the shallots over a medium heat for 3–4 minutes until softened, making sure the shallots do not brown as this could give the sauce a bitter flavour. Cut the passion fruit in half, scoop out the flesh and add to the pan, stirring it into the shallots. Reduce the heat to low, stir in the mustard and then the lime juice, followed by the cream. Bubble until the sauce reduces by half, stirring constantly. Add half the coriander (cilantro) leaves and season with salt and pepper.

Add the cooked lobster to the sauce or pour the sauce over the lobster meat. Serve garnished with the remaining coriander leaves and the finely grated lime zest.

BISQUE OF CANADIAN LOBSTER

STARTER, LUNCH — SERVES 4
PREPARATION **1 HOUR 25 MINUTES** — COOKING **1 HOUR**

Lobsters only turn red when you cook them. Live lobsters are a dark colour, usually green or reddish brown, which camouflages them on the seabed. This is due to the pigments they absorb from plankton (carotenoids), which bind with the proteins in their shells. When you cook a lobster, these pigments are released so the lobster reverts to its characteristic bright red colour. The shells of lobsters and other crustaceans contain elements such as pigments, proteins and sugars that add flavour so don't throw the shells away! Use them to make rich sauces and soups like this bisque but, watch out, the pigments dissolve more quickly in oil than in water. To ensure your soup is a luscious red colour, first fry the shells in a good splash of oil.

INGREDIENTS

2 x 500–600-g/1 lb 2-oz–1 lb
   5-oz live lobsters
2 litres/3½ pints/8½ cups court
   bouillon (see page 392), or
   enough to cover the lobsters,
   or salted water
1 onion, sliced
1 leek, trimmed, cut into rings
   and green parts removed
½ fennel bulb, sliced
2 garlic cloves, finely chopped
5 tbsp tomato purée (paste)
150 ml/5 fl oz/⅔ cup Cognac
200 ml/7 fl oz/scant 1 cup
   white wine
1 litre/1 ¾ pints/4¼ cups fish
   stock (see page 390)
bouquet garni (sprigs of flat-leaf
   parsley and thyme with 1 bay
   leaf, tied together with thin
   string)
¼ tsp ground piment
   d'Espelette
3 tbsp double (heavy) cream
groundnut (peanut) oil
salt and pepper

Put the lobsters in the freezer for 1 hour to render them unconscious. Remove from the freezer and leave for 15 minutes to come to room temperature. Bring the court bouillon or salted water to the boil in a large pan, add the lobsters and boil for 8 minutes. Drain and lightly rinse them under cold running water. Break off the tails and remove the meat. Crack the claws and dig out the meat with a lobster pick (see page 403). Set the meat aside. With a large knife, bash the shells of the lobster heads, short legs and body into rough pieces.

Heat 3 tablespoons of groundnut (peanut) oil in a deep, heavy frying pan (skillet) over a high heat and fry the lobster shells for 5 minutes. Add the onion, leek and fennel and fry for another 5 minutes, stirring frequently. Add the garlic and tomato purée (paste) after 30 seconds and then sauté for 1 minute, stirring constantly. Deglaze the pan with the Cognac, add the white wine and then pour in the stock. Add the bouquet garni and piment d'Espelette, mixing well. Season with salt and pepper, cover the pan with a lid and simmer over a low heat for 30–40 minutes.

Meanwhile cut the lobster meat into rough chunks.

Remove the bouquet garni from the pan and strain the bisque through a conical sieve (strainer). If you don't have a conical sieve, use a potato masher to break up the lobster shells and then strain through an ordinary round sieve.

Return the strained bisque to a clean saucepan and place over a high heat. Add the lobster meat and heat for 2 minutes. Lift out the meat, add the cream to the pan and stir over the heat for 2 minutes.

Divide the lobster meat between serving plates and ladle the bisque over the top.

FRIED SCALLOPS
WITH SEA VEGETABLES

MAIN COURSE — SERVES 4
PREPARATION **5 MINUTES** — COOKING **10 MINUTES**

Bay scallops – what the French call coquilles St Jacques – are the most popular shellfish in Nova Scotia after lobster and crab. You can find these beautiful shells at depths up to 100 metres (328 feet) – or more – between Cape Hatteras and Labrador where the fisheries have been MSC-certified since 2010.

INGREDIENTS

20 scallops (North American sea scallops), removed from their shells
1 garlic clove, peeled and left whole
25 g/1 oz/2 tbsp butter
½ shallot, chopped
150 g/5 oz sea lavender
juice of ¼ lemon
groundnut (peanut) oil, for frying
salt and pepper

ALTERNATIVE TO SEA LAVENDER

marsh samphire (sea asparagus/ sea beans)

Pat the scallops dry with kitchen paper (paper towels) and season them on both sides with salt and pepper. Heat 4 tablespoons of the groundnut (peanut) oil in a frying pan (skillet) over a high heat. Place the scallops in the pan in a single layer and, depending on their thickness, turn them over after 2–3 minutes. Fry for another 2–3 minutes to brown the other sides, without moving the scallops around in the pan. Once nicely browned, remove the scallops from the pan and keep warm covered with foil or in the oven on its lowest setting.

Spear the garlic clove on the prongs of a fork. Heat the butter in a saucepan over a medium heat and fry the shallot for 2 minutes until translucent. Season lightly with a pinch of pepper. Add the sea lavender and stir with the garlic-topped fork for 1–2 minutes so it is infused with the flavour of the garlic and has softened. Add the lemon juice and check the seasoning, adding salt and pepper to taste.

Serve the scallops with the sea lavender and the buttery juices spooned over.

SCALLOPS IN CHIVE CREAM WITH HERRING & SALMON CAVIAR

STARTER — SERVES 4
COOKING 20 MINUTES

There are so many ways to enjoy scallops; raw, seared, marinated, poached. I love all the soft textures and silky flavours of this dish when combined with the crispy, salty roe.

INGREDIENTS

25 g/1 oz/2 tbsp butter
1 onion, finely chopped
1 leek, trimmed and finely sliced
1 carrot, finely sliced
100 ml/3½ fl oz/generous ⅓ cup white wine
300 ml/10 fl oz/1¼ cups fish stock (see page 390)
12 scallops (North American sea scallops), removed from their shells
1 egg yolk
100 ml/3½ fl oz/generous ⅓ cup double (heavy) cream
handful of chives, finely chopped
1 tbsp herring roe from a jar
2 tbsp salmon caviar (keta) from a jar
1 tbsp beet sprouts
1 tbsp lemon cress (lemon basil)
salt and pepper

Heat the butter in a frying pan (skillet) or large saucepan, add the onion, leek and carrot and fry for 2 minutes until softened, but not browned. Deglaze with the white wine. Let the liquid bubble over a medium-high heat until reduced by two-thirds. Add the stock and simmer gently until the liquid has reduced by half.

Poach the scallops in the liquid over a low heat for 3–5 minutes, depending on their thickness. If the scallops are not completely immersed in the liquid, turn them over halfway. Lift the scallops out of the pan and cover them with foil to keep warm.

Strain the cooking liquid into a clean pan. Whisk the egg yolk and cream together in a bowl. Return the liquid to the heat and bring back to the boil. When boiling, reduce the heat to low and whisk in the egg and cream mixture. Heat the sauce without letting it boil again, add the chives and season with salt and pepper.

Divide the scallops between four deep plates and pour the soup over. Using a small teaspoon, divide the herring roe and salmon caviar between the servings. Garnish with beet sprouts and lemon cress (lemon basil).

KOREAN FISH PANCAKE

CANAPÉ, STARTER, LUNCH — SERVES 4
PREPARATION **5 MINUTES** — COOKING **20 MINUTES**

Savoury pancakes are served in bars all over South Korea, chopped by the chef into bite-size pieces that can be picked up with chopsticks and dipped into a sauce. Often served with an unfiltered rice wine called makgeolli that can be blended with fruit and ice for a cooling cocktail. You can make fish pancakes with any fish species or cooked seafood so long as you use the base of spring onion (scallion).

INGREDIENTS

DIP

2 tbsp soy sauce
2 tbsp fish sauce
25 g/1 oz/2 tbsp sugar
1 tbsp lemon juice
1 tbsp rice vinegar
½ garlic clove, crushed
½ red chilli (chile), deseeded
   and finely chopped

PANCAKES

1 tbsp white sesame seeds
250 g/9 oz/1¾ cups plain
   (all-purpose) flour
250 ml/8 fl oz/1 cup cold water
2 eggs, beaten
4 scallops (North American sea
   scallops), removed from their
   shells
4 squid, cleaned (see page 401)
   and cut into small pieces
4 large prawns (shrimp), peeled
12 spring onions (scallions), cut
   into 4-cm/1½-inch lengths
2 red (bell) peppers, deseeded and diced, plus extra for
   garnish
2 jalapeño chillies (chiles),
   sliced, plus extra for garnish
handful of coriander (cilantro),
   leaves pulled from their stalks
½ red chilli (chile), thinly sliced
sunflower oil, for frying
salt
lime halves, to serve

To make the dip, put the soy sauce, fish sauce and sugar in a pan over a low heat and stir until the sugar has dissolved. Allow to cool and then add the lemon juice, rice vinegar and 1 tablespoon of water. Finally, stir in the garlic and chilli (chile).

Roast the sesame seeds for 1–2 minutes in a dry frying pan (skillet) over a medium-high heat until golden. Remove from the pan and set aside.

To make the pancakes, sift the flour into a large bowl. To avoid lumps forming, whisk the water into the flour a little at a time before whisking in the eggs to make a smooth batter. Finally add a pinch of salt.

Add the scallops, squid and prawns (shrimp) to the batter, stirring the seafood in quickly but thoroughly so all the pieces are well coated. This amount of batter is enough to make two large pancakes.

Heat a little sunflower oil in a large frying pan (skillet) over a medium heat and add half the spring onions (scallions), the (bell) peppers and the jalapeño chillies. Fry for 1 minute until the vegetables have softened and become slightly translucent. Add half the batter to the pan and give it a gentle shake so the pancake will slide out easily when it is cooked. Lower the heat, cover the pan with a lid and fry for 4–6 minutes, turning the pancake over once it has set underneath. Fry the other side for 1 minute and then remove the pancake from the pan and keep it warm in a low oven (100°C/200°F/Gas Mark ¼) or cover with foil. Fry a second pancake in the same way.

Scatter over the coriander (cilantro) leaves, jalapeño and red chilli slices and roasted sesame seeds. Cut each pancake in half and then into smaller pieces. Serve with the dip and lime halves to squeeze over.

GETARIA

MADRID

SPAIN

ANCHOVIES
&
OCTOPUS

GETERIA, SPAIN — 43°18'27.2"N 2°12'09.6"W
FAO 21 ATLANTIC OCEAN NE
FISHERMEN — JUANJO & ANDRES

FISHING FOR ANCHOVIES WITH THE ENTIRE FAMILY

— 🦑 —

As soon as you see women walking along the quays carrying chairs with short legs you know that a fishing boat is about to enter harbour. Once the crates of anchovies have been unloaded, the net is hoisted ashore to be cleaned. A dozen or so fishermen stand in a semicircle on the quay shaking the net to remove the debris as they haul it in, risking showering anyone walking underneath with bits of fish and dead crabs.

Directly behind the fishermen, the women squat down on their low chairs. They are virtually sitting on the ground, with their legs stretched out in front of them and a cushion under their ankles. Their sewing materials are in a small case and their scissors dangle around their necks. The men tie ribbons in the net to indicate where it needs repairing and, after shaking it clean, pile it up in a mound some 2 metres/6½ feet tall with dozens of the ribbons blowing in the wind. It may take the women all weekend to make sure the net is ready for use again on Monday morning.

Anchovy fishing in Spain's Basque country is still essentially a family affair. The women mending the nets are often the wives and mothers of the fishermen, and the boats are also family-owned. Juanjo Azkue Aranguren is skipper of the *Santa María*. Along with two cousins and his wife's brother, he is also the boat's owner, having taken it over from his father and uncles. As far as he knows, his family have always been fishermen.

All the boat owners operating in the harbour form a *cofradía* (meaning 'brotherhood' or fraternity) to represent their interests, a system dating back over a century. In 1986, the five *cofradías* of the Basque coastal province of Guipúzcoa joined up with various manufacturers and fish processors to form a federation, and early in 2015, together with the fisheries of two neighbouring provinces, they received MSC certification.

The Basques fish for anchovies with small purse seine boats. A net is deployed from the boat, which sails around an entire school of fish, encircling them with the net. When the bottom of the net is drawn tight, the fish are caught, as though in a basket. There is virtually no bycatch involved with this technique as anchovy always swim in compact schools, making fishing for them highly selective.

It also allows to the fishermen to check the size of the anchovies before hauling them in. If the fish are too small (there should be no more than 90 per kilo/2 lb 4 oz, which is the official limit), the net is opened and the anchovies are allowed to swim away. Sometimes the anchovies dive deeper into the ocean and then purse seiners are unable to get near them with the net. Pelagic trawlers, boats that are drag their large nets further out and deeper in the ocean, are unable to be as selective and collect all the fish in a single location – large and small – in a single catch.

While the catch is still being hoisted ashore, potential buyers at the auction house are already examining the first crate. The anchovies are divided according to quantity per kilo. Today, the *Santa María* has two sizes to offer: 99 crates of 46 ale (46 fish per kilo) and 55 crates of 31 ale. The latter are the size of sardines and are all practically identical, which is what fish dealers like to see. They also like the fish to be shiny, with no redness around the gills and no damage to the eyes and bellies. It looks as if the *Santa María's* crew have been extra careful with their fish as these anchovies are perfect.

Spain's Basque country, and San Sebastian in particular, is famous for its rich culinary heritage. Michelin-starred restaurants such as Arzak and Mugaritz have a worldwide reputation and there's a *pintxos* bar on every street corner (the Basque version of tapas). But gastronomic traditions go even further as everyone cooks. The fishermen take over the kitchen at weekends since they are members of a *sociedad gastronómica*, a traditional cooking club that only men were allowed to join originally and where sons learned to cook from their fathers. Today, these clubs are social places for entire families to get together for lunch and dinner, dining at long tables.

Bottles of beer and *txacoli* (a local dry sparkling wine similar to cider) are chilling in the fridge and there's a crate by every table. At the end of the night the empty bottles are counted and bills are settled. Everyone who eats helps out in the kitchen but the cooks must be careful. If they want to remain on good terms with their fellow diners, they must follow the traditional recipes absolutely precisely. The anchovies are grilled (broiled) with garlic and sea salt and nothing else. It's a matter of tradition and pride.

BOQUERONES & TOMATO BREAD

CANAPÉ, STARTER — SERVES 4
PREPARATION 5 HOURS 10 MINUTES — COOKING 10 MINUTES

The anchovy is a small yet incredibly versatile fish. It can be salted, and/or cured in brine, marinated and fermented. Originally these methods were ways of preserving the fish but although that is less important these days, they are still used to create a wide range of different flavours. Pickled anchovies are best known as Spanish boquerones en vinagre. The fillets are lightly salted and then marinated in vinegar for a couple of hours, or in a mixture of oil and vinegar. The acid in the vinegar 'cooks' the flesh of the fish making it soft, white and tasty. And on a different subject entirely – a high amount of acidity (either in a marinade or a poaching fluid) helps stop the smell of fish permeating the kitchen and the rest of the house.

INGREDIENTS

BOQUERONES

175 g/6 oz fresh anchovy fillets
150 ml/5 fl oz/²/³ cup white
   wine vinegar
3 tbsp extra virgin olive oil
1 garlic clove, finely chopped
2 sprigs of flat-leaf parsley,
   finely chopped
pepper

TOMATO BREAD

½ white baguette
2 large ripe tomatoes, halved
2 x 50-g (2-oz) cans of anchovy
   fillets in olive oil, drained
extra virgin olive oil for drizzling

To prepare the boquerones, lay the anchovy fillets on a plate, skin-side up, and grind over a little pepper. Pour the vinegar over the fillets until they are just covered and leave to marinate in the refrigerator for 4 hours.

Lift the fillets from the marinade, rinse them lightly under cold running water and pat dry with kitchen paper (paper towels). Mix the olive oil with the garlic and parsley in a bowl. Arrange the fillets on a plate and pour over the garlic oil. Cover tightly with cling film (plastic wrap) and leave to marinate in the refrigerator for at least 1 hour.

Take the anchovy fillets out of the refrigerator 15 minutes before you are ready to serve them, so they have time to come to room temperature and any oil that has solidified can dissolve again.

To make the tomato bread, preheat the oven to 200°C/400°F/Gas Mark 6.

Halve the baguette lengthwise and cut each half into 5–8=cm/2–3-inch slices. Toast the bread on a rack in the oven, cut-sides up, for 3–5 minutes until the slices are golden brown. Remove from the oven and leave to cool.

Rub the cut sides of the tomatoes over the bread as though you were 'grating' the tomato onto it. Divide the canned anchovy fillets between the bread slices and drizzle with olive oil.

FRIED ANCHOVIES
IN GARLIC

LUNCH, MAIN COURSE — SERVES 4
PREPARATION 10 MINUTES — COOKING 10 MINUTES

I first made this dish at a fishermen's society. After a day of fishing the fishermen go to a private club where they cook the fish they have just caught in a very simple Spanish way. This version combines fresh fish, bread and lettuce to serve with a good glass of Txakolina, a type of lightly sparkling wine. Simple is best. Simple pleasure.

INGREDIENTS

800 g/1 lb 12 oz whole fresh
    anchovies
50 g/2 oz/scant ½ cup plain
    (all-purpose) flour
2 garlic cloves, thinly sliced
1 lettuce, separated into leaves
    and rinsed
1 white onion, thinly sliced
1 white baguette
light olive oil, for frying
extra virgin olive oil and sherry
    vinegar, to serve
salt and pepper

Remove the heads and clean the anchovies with your thumb or a small knife. Rinse them lightly under cold running water and pat dry with kitchen paper (paper towels). Sift the flour onto a plate and season with salt and pepper. Roll the fish in the flour, shaking off any excess, until they are thinly and evenly coated.

Heat 3 tablespoons of the light olive oil in a frying pan (skillet) over a high heat. When the oil is very hot, fry the anchovies in batches, adding just enough to cover the base of the pan and taking care not to overfill it. Fry each batch on both sides for 2–3 minutes, adding a little of the garlic each time halfway. Drain the anchovies and garlic from the pan once the anchovies have a crisp crust.

Transfer the anchovies and garlic to a platter or serving dish. Mix the lettuce and sliced onion in a bowl and follow the Spanish custom of placing bottles of extra virgin olive oil and sherry vinegar on the table for your guests to dress the lettuce themselves.

Accompany with crusty baguettes.

LINGUINE WITH ANCHOVIES, ALMONDS & SAGE

STARTER, LUNCH — SERVES 4
COOKING 15 MINUTES

Everyone is familiar with salted anchovies in cans but, in the Mediterranean, cooks have used salted anchovies to enhance the flavour of dishes for centuries. The fish fillets are liberally salted, packed in pressurized containers and left to mature for up to 10 months. As they are stored at a fairly high temperature (15–30°C/59–86°F), bacteria and enzymes in the fish begin to produce all manner of complex aromas. If you concentrate, you can detect hints of mushroom, meat, butter, sugar and even fruits or flowers, mixed with the fish. Salted anchovies dissolve easily in sauces and other dishes.

INGREDIENTS

400 g/14 oz linguine (or any dried pasta of your choice)
100 g/4 oz/²/₃ cup whole blanched almonds
20 g/³/₄ oz/1 ½ tbsp butter
handful of sage leaves, finely chopped
1 x 50-g (2-oz) can of anchovy fillets in olive oil, drained
extra virgin olive oil, for frying and drizzling
salt and pepper

Boil the pasta in a large pan of lightly salted water until al dente. Just before the pasta is ready, spoon 1 tablespoon of the cooking water into a cup and set aside. Drain the pasta in a colander and mix with a little olive oil to prevent it sticking together.

Heat 1 tablespoon of olive oil in a large frying pan (skillet) over medium-high heat and fry the almonds for about 1 minute, stirring constantly until they are golden brown. Add the butter and half the sage.

Mash half the anchovy fillets with a fork, add to the pan and cook for a further 1 minute. Add the pasta and the reserved pasta water and toss everything together. Season with pepper – extra salt is not necessary as the anchovies are already quite salty. Serve garnished with the rest of the anchovy fillets and sage, drizzled with extra olive oil.

OCTOPUS SALAD

CANAPÉ, STARTER, LUNCH — SERVES 4
PREPARATION 5 MINUTES — COOKING 1 HOUR

A little over 4 hours' drive from Getaria – where local fishermen catch their anchovies – is Puerto de Vega, a beautiful place that boasts the only recently MSC-certified sustainable octopus fishery in the world. In this artisan fishery they catch octopus using pots close to the shore, and as an example of their responsible approach to fishing, any octopus that weighs less than 1 kg/2 lb 4 oz is put back in the water.

INGREDIENTS

400 g/14 oz octopus tentacles, rinsed
1 celery stick, finely chopped
1 bay leaf
1 tbsp extra virgin olive oil
1 tbsp black olives, pitted
200 g/7 oz 'Christmas grapes' tomatoes (or another variety of cherry tomato), quartered
handful of flat-leaf parsley, finely chopped
salt and pepper

Fill a saucepan with plenty of cold water and add a pinch of salt, the octopus tentacles, celery and bay leaf. Bring to the boil and simmer for 30 minutes. Remove from the heat and leave the octopus in the water for a further 30 minutes. Drain the octopus and celery from the pan.

Skin the octopus and cut into pieces. Leave to cool until lukewarm, reserving the celery.

Put the octopus in a bowl with the olive oil, olives, tomatoes, reserved celery and parsley. Season with salt and pepper and mix well.

Spoon the salad onto a serving platter and accompany with good country bread.

GRILLED OCTOPUS IN AN AVOCADO & OLIVE SAUCE

MAIN COURSE — SERVES 4
PREPARATION 15 MINUTES — COOKING 1 HOUR 10 MINUTES

To give the boiled octopus a lovely charred flavour, grill it over hot coals or in a smoking hot grill pan.

INGREDIENTS

OCTOPUS

2 celery sticks, coarsely chopped
1 lemon, cut in half
3 bay leaves
5 sprigs of thyme
10 black peppercorns
1 octopus, weighing 1–1.5 kg/2 lb 4 oz–3 lb 6 oz

SAUCE

1 egg yolk
2 tbsp lime juice
200 ml/7 fl oz/scant 1 cup sunflower oil
100 ml/3½ fl oz/generous ⅓ cup olive oil
20 Kalamata olives (or another variety of black olive), pitted
Worcestershire sauce
salt and pepper

AVOCADO & TOMATOES

4 avocados
paprika
10 'Christmas grapes' tomatoes (or another variety of cherry tomato), halved
½ bunch of coriander (cilantro) leaves
1 lime, cut into wedges
coarse sea salt (optional)

To cook the octopus, put the celery, lemon, bay leaves, thyme and black peppercorns in a large pan of cold water and bring to the boil.

Meanwhile, wash the octopus under cold running water, turning the mantle inside out and rinsing well.

Reduce the heat slightly under the pan so the water comes off the boil. Immerse the octopus tentacles slowly in and out of the water to avoid a sudden 'plunge'. Repeat several times and then place the whole octopus in the water, cover the pan and cook for 30–40 minutes. Remove the lid from the pan and turn off the heat, leaving the octopus in the water for a further 20–25 minutes.

Drain the octopus, pierce it with the tip of a knife to check it is tender, before cutting the tentacles into roughly 5-cm/2-inch pieces. Set aside.

To make the sauce, combine the egg yolk with the lime juice in a blender or food processor. With the motor running, add the sunflower oil in drops, followed by the olive oil, processing until you have a smooth mayonnaise. Add the olives and process again until smooth and incorporated into the mayonnaise. Season with Worcestershire sauce, salt and pepper. Set aside.

To prepare the avocados, halve them and remove the stones (pits). Using a tablespoon, scoop out the flesh from each half, keeping it in one piece. Cut the flesh lengthwise into 5-mm/¼-inch slices.

Heat a grill pan (broiler pan) over a high heat. Once the pan is hot, grill (broil) the avocado slices on both sides for 2–3 minutes, or until they start to caramelize. Clean the pan and sprinkle a little paprika over the octopus tentacles. Grill the tentacles – having first sprinkled them with a little olive oil, if wished – until they are a rich caramel colour. This will take only a few minutes, so keep an eye on the pan and turn the tentacles over occasionally. Add the tomato halves when the tentacles are almost ready. Cook for around 30 seconds.

Serve the grilled octopus with the avocado, tomatoes and olive sauce in a serving dish or on a platter. Drizzle with a little olive oil and garnish with the coriander (cilantro) leaves and lime wedges and sprinkle with a little coarse sea salt.

INDIA

CLAMS

KOLLAM, INDIA — 8°56'59.7"N 76°33'19.6"E
FAO 51 INDIAN OCEAN W
FISHERMEN — SILVI & FAMILY

THE BEST CLAMS
ARE DREDGED
BY FOOT

—— ⬭ ——

First light marks the start of the day for clam fishermen in Kollam, and once the sun rises above the horizon, the working day starts in earnest. The light must be shining directly into the water so the divers can see the clams lying submerged on the bottom. Kollam is by Lake Ashtamudi, one of the largest estuaries in India's southwest province of Kerala. The lake is fed by water from the Kallada river and most of the lake is fresh water apart from the narrow opening to the Indian Ocean where it is brackish. It is here that they fish for short-neck (carpet shell) clams, small shellfish that are a particular delicacy in Asia and full of flavour.

Silvi Thomas lives with his family on St Sebastian, one of the lake's many small islands. In the morning he takes out a canoe he made himself from a hollowed-out tree trunk and paddles out into the lake. Equipped with a scoop net on a long stick and a rake Silvi dives without oxygen into the water, sometimes to a depth of 3–4 metres/10–13 feet. He kicks the clams loose from the sand and hops backwards onto the lake's bed, raking the clams into his net. After emptying his net into the canoe, he dives back down again. The clam divers of Kollam are superb athletes and can do this for 4–5 hours. Some of the divers can hold their breath for minutes at a time. On a good day a single fisherman can catch as much as 200 kg/440 lb like this.

There are around a thousand clam divers like Silvi in Kollam. The fishery provides employment for at least four thousand people and it's a real family affair. When their canoes are full, the divers return home where they keep the clams submerged in crates filled with water for 6–8 hours, during which time the molluscs clean themselves by expelling sand from their shells. The clams are then tipped onto a sheet spread out inside the house and the entire family gather round. Wives, grandmothers and children all sit down to extract the clams, one by one, from their shells. They do this at an incredible speed, using their fingers or an empty shell.

Clams are not the only sea creatures that are fished in Lake Ashtamudi. Further out they catch crab, shrimp, other shellfish and sardines but these are just for local consumption. It is only clams that are fished in Kollam on a proper commercial basis. They are mainly exported to Japan, where they are extremely popular. With a bit of luck maybe we'll soon be able to enjoy these gorgeous clams in Europe, too.

Commercial clam fishing began in the 1980s, when the demand in Malaysia, Thailand and Vietnam started to grow at a great rate. Business was booming until the 1990s when overfishing led to a steep decline in the catch. Since then measures have been taken to maintain sustainability. The mesh in the nets is now wider, a minimum size of clam has been set for export and fishing is suspended between December and February when the clams spawn.

The main reason that shellfish in Kollam are doing much better is that mechanical fishing is now prohibited. Today, divers are fishing in the traditional way once more, loosening them with their feet, and, in 2014, the Ashtamudi clam fishery became the first MSC-certified fishery in India. Each year around 10,000 tonnes of clams are caught in the lake without putting them under any undue pressure. After the clams have been extracted from their shells, they are collected by dealers who take boats packed with ice to the islands, and go from house to house. The shelled clams are sorted and weighed at a central point; the fewer there are per kilo, the higher the price. The clams are then frozen and shipped to Vietnam or Japan (and hopefully Europe, soon).

The next day, once the sun has risen high enough, the whole process starts again, but not all fisherman dive. A few years ago, some of them began using a kind of grabber that looks like two nets on a long stick. They use it to scoop up clams from the bed of the lake from on board a boat. It saves a lot of hard work, but there are still plenty of people like Silvi Thomas who continue to dive in the traditional way and the effort brings its own reward. You can be a lot more selective when you are underwater than when you are scooping up clams from on board a boat. Silvi Thomas brings only the largest clams up to the surface and they fetch the highest price.

KERALAN SHORT-NECK (CARPET SHELL) CLAM CURRY

STARTER, LUNCH — SERVES 4
COOKING **20 MINUTES**

This is a dish I made with Mr Silvi and his family all together one afternoon. We cooked the fresh catch with locally produced Marsala which I particularly enjoyed. The base cooks for a little while before you add the clams and we ate it at sunset on the sandbank.

INGREDIENTS

1 kg/2 lb 4 oz short-neck (carpet shell) clams, washed
6 tbsp coconut oil
2 red onions, roughly chopped
2 red chillies (chiles), roughly chopped
2 green chillies (chiles), roughly chopped
2 garlic cloves, finely chopped
12 fresh, dried or frozen curry leaves, plus extra for garnish if using fresh
2-cm/¾-inch piece of fresh root ginger, peeled and finely chopped
2 tsp ground turmeric
1 tbsp chilli powder
4 tsp ground coriander
2 tomatoes, cut into wedges
pepper

ALTERNATIVE SEAFOOD

any kind of shellfish

Check the clam shells carefully and discard any that are broken.

Heat the coconut oil in a large pan over a medium heat and sauté the red onions, red and green chillies (chiles) and the garlic for 5 minutes, adding the curry leaves and ginger as soon as the vegetables begin to brown. Reduce the heat and cook for another couple of minutes. Add the turmeric, chilli powder and coriander and stir well. After 2 minutes, add the tomato wedges and season with black pepper.

Stir well, add the clams and cover the pan with a lid. Cook the clams for 4–6 minutes, giving the mixture an occasional stir. The dish is ready as soon as all the shells have opened.

Serve the clams in a bowl, garnished with fresh curry leaves.

POLLICHATHU
FISH IN BANANA LEAVES

MAIN COURSE — SERVES 4
PREPARATION 15 MINUTES — COOKING 35 MINUTES

One of the most popular dishes among the fishing communities of Kerala is karimeen pollichathu. You can see the karimeen fish, known in English as pearl spot, in the photo opposite. It is common in Lake Ashtamudi and is considered a delicacy in India, but you can use any medium-sized whole fish, such as red mullet or whiting. The secret is to rub the marinade all over each fish and then wrap each one in a banana leaf with the masala spice mixture. The banana leaves protect the fish while they are being cooked and also add a nice fresh flavour. Searing the leaves briefly first makes them more flexible and easier to wrap around the fish, as well as improving the taste.

INGREDIENTS

MARINADE

1 tbsp chilli powder
2 tsp ground turmeric
juice of 2 lemons
4 x 300–400-g/10–14-oz whole round fish, such as mullet
coconut oil for frying
salt

MASALA

3-cm/1¼-inch piece of fresh root ginger, peeled and finely chopped
125 ml/4 fl oz/8 tbsp coconut oil
1 tsp mustard seeds
2 tsp fennel seeds
4 tsp finely chopped garlic
2 tsp finely chopped green chillies (chiles)
handful of fresh or frozen curry leaves
3 onions, chopped
2 tsp chilli powder
2 tsp ground turmeric
6 tomatoes, thinly sliced
6 tbsp coconut milk
4 banana leaves, each large enough to enclose a fish
1 onion, sliced
2 tomatoes, roughly chopped
1 lime, sliced

ALTERNATIVE SHELLFISH

mullet or whiting

To make the marinade, in a bowl, mix together the chilli powder, ground turmeric, lemon juice and salt to taste. Stir in 1 tablespoon of cold water.

To prepare the fish, clean the fish (see page 398). With a sharp knife, make cuts 1.5 cm/⅔ inch apart into the flesh on each side and, wearing thin, plastic gloves, rub the marinade all over the fish.

Heat a little coconut oil in a frying pan (skillet) over a high heat and fry the fish for 4–6 minutes on each side until browned. Drain from the pan and set aside. If using the same pan to make the masala, wash and dry it.

To make the masala, put the ginger, coconut oil, mustard seeds, fennel seeds, garlic, green chillies (chiles), curry leaves and chopped onions in a frying pan and fry for 2 minutes. Add the chilli powder, ground turmeric and tomatoes and season with salt. Cook for 10–15 minutes over a low heat, stirring occasionally until the mixture is thick and smooth. Add the coconut milk and cook for a further 1–2 minutes.

To assemble the parcels, hold one side of each banana leaf over a gas flame (or use a chef's blow torch) for a few seconds to soften it. Divide half of the masala between the four leaves, place the fish on top and, reserving 1 tablespoon, spread the rest of the masala over the fish. Fold the banana leaves around the fish to make four parcels, tying them up securely with thin string. Fry the parcels in a dry frying pan for 2 minutes on each side over a medium-high heat.

Cook the sliced onion and tomatoes for 2 minutes in a pan with the reserved tablespoon of masala.

Open the banana leaves and serve the fish immediately with the onion and tomato mixture spooned on top. Top each with a slice of lime.

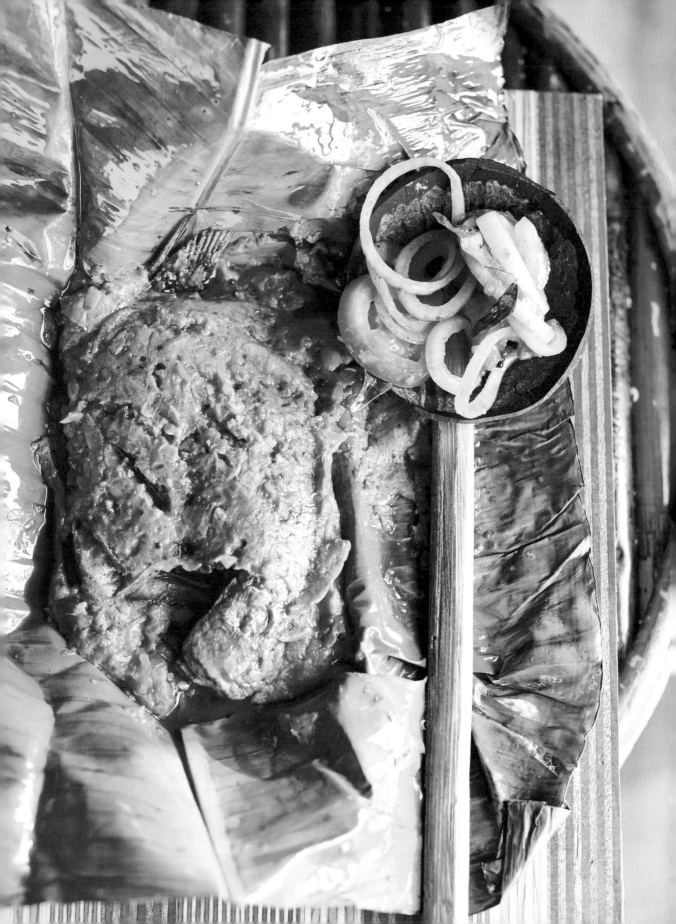

PASTA WITH COCKLES & WHITE WINE

STARTER, LUNCH — SERVES 4
COOKING 15 MINUTES

Pasta alla vongole! How often have you seen this dish on a menu and not just in an Italian restaurant? But what are vongole? Vongole is the Italian word for some – though not all – venus clams. A single mollusc is called a vongola and a golden venus clam goes by the evocative name of vongola gialla. Vongole can also refer to vongole telline, a very small variety of clam, but usually when you get clams in pasta, they are vongole veraci, also part of the venus clam family. Pasta alla vongole can be made with cockles as, although clams are firmer and have slightly more bite, cockles are juicier with a more delicate flavour. They make an excellent pasta dish such as this linguine cocciole.

INGREDIENTS

400 g/14 oz linguine or spaghetti (or another dried pasta of your choice)
handful of flat-leaf parsley, stalks and leaves separated
1 shallot, chopped
½ red chilli (chile), deseeded and finely chopped
1 garlic clove, finely chopped
4 tbsp white wine
1 kg/2 lb 4 oz cockles, washed
12 cherry tomatoes, quartered
olive oil
salt and pepper

ALTERNATIVE SHELLFISH

clams or baby clams

Cook the pasta in a large pan of lightly salted water until it is al dente.

Meanwhile, crush the parsley stalks with a heavy knife on a chopping board until they split to enhance their flavour. Cut the stalks into small pieces and finely chop the leaves.

Heat 2 tablespoons of olive oil in a frying pan (skillet) over a medium-high heat and add the shallot and chilli (chile). Fry for 2 minutes until the shallot is translucent and softened. Add the garlic, fry for 1 minute and then add the parsley stalks. Deglaze the pan with the white wine. As soon as the wine bubbles, add the cockles and tomatoes and cover the pan with a lid. Turn the heat down to low. Shake the pan and lift the lid regularly to check if the cockle shells have opened. Add the chopped parsley leaves after 3 minutes.

Once all the shells have opened – this will take 4–6 minutes – immediately take the pan off the heat. Taste the cooking liquid and season with salt and pepper but avoid adding too much salt as cockles are naturally quite salty.

Drain the pasta and add it to the cockles. Toss well and serve with another pinch of black pepper sprinkled over.

CHOWDER

Chowder is a traditional soup from America's north-eastern states. Opinions differ as to the precise recipe but it's always thick and usually quite pale in colour due to the addition of milk or cream and potatoes (in some areas a tomato is added as well). Corn chowder is especially popular but by far the best known, and the oldest, is clam chowder. The English word chowder probably derives from the French chaudière, a type of iron cooking pot that French colonists took with them they settled in eastern Canada. Micmacs, the First Nations people of the area, ate huge quantities of clams, cooking them on hot stones in hollowed out tree trunks filled with water. The first chowder, therefore, seems to have been a combination of a local recipe and a French cooking method.

INGREDIENTS

400 g/14 oz cockles, cleaned
25 g/1 oz/2 tbsp butter
80 g/3¼ oz pancetta, diced
1 onion, chopped
2 celery sticks, finely chopped
250 g/9 oz potatoes, peeled and diced
800 ml/1 pint 7 fl oz/3⅓ cups fish stock (see page 390)
2 bay leaves
2 sprigs of thyme, plus extra for garnish
200 ml/7 fl oz/scant 1 cup milk
pepper

ALTERNATIVE SHELLFISH

clams or baby clams

Check to see if all the cockle shells are whole and discard any broken ones. Cook the cockles in a covered pan in a small amount of water for 3 minutes. Lift out the cockles as soon as the shells have opened and strain the liquid left in the pan into a large bowl. Remove the meat from half the shells, reserving the rest in the shells for garnish. Set the cockle meat and shells to one side on a plate.

Add the butter to the pan over a medium-high heat, followed by the pancetta, onion and celery. Fry over a low heat for 5 minutes until the onion is translucent and the fat in the pancetta has melted. Add the diced potatoes and cook for a further 1 minute. Add the cockle broth, fish stock, bay leaves and thyme and cook for 8–10 minutes over a medium-high heat until the potatoes are tender. Reduce the heat to low and add the milk.

Season the soup with pepper. It might not be necessary to add salt as the pancetta and cockles are already quite salty. Simmer the soup over a low heat for 5 minutes before serving.

Divide the cockle meat and shells between four soup bowls and ladle in the soup – the hot liquid will heat up the cockles. Serve garnished with thyme sprigs.

FREGOLA WITH CLAMS IN TOMATO SAUCE

STARTER, LUNCH — SERVES 4
COOKING 20 MINUTES

The first time I ate this dish was at Chioggia, which is next to the laguna in Venice where they catch wonderful vongole (clams). This dish is inspired by that memory of fishing for vongole with the amazing city of Venice in the background and combines classic Italian flavours with its freshest seafood.

INGREDIENTS

300 g/10 oz fregola (or any other dried pasta of your choice)
2 garlic cloves, sliced
½ red chilli (chile), thinly sliced
1 kg/2 lb 4 oz clams, cleaned
3 tbsp white wine
4 tbsp canned plum tomatoes, puréed
handful of flat-leaf parsley, finely chopped
extra virgin olive oil, for drizzling and frying
salt and pepper

ALTERNATIVE SHELLFISH

cockles

Cook the fregola for 10 minutes in a large pan of lightly salted boiling water. Drain and add a drizzle of olive oil to prevent the fregola sticking together.

Heat 2 tablespoons of olive oil in a frying pan (skillet) over a medium-high heat and sauté the garlic and chilli (chile) without letting them brown. After 2 minutes add the clams and deglaze the pan with the white wine. As soon as the wine starts to bubble, add the puréed tomatoes, cover the pan and leave the clams to simmer until their shells have opened. Add the parsley and fregola and heat through thoroughly.

Drizzle over a little olive oil, grind over some black pepper and serve straight from the pan.

CLAMS EN PAPILLOTE

CANAPÉ, STARTER — SERVES 4
PREPARATION 10 MINUTES — COOKING 15 MINUTES

The term 'clam' includes a wide range of shellfish and it's not always clear which type is being referred to. The confusion is understandable as 'clam' encompasses all kinds of bivalve molluscs. Strictly speaking, it should be used only for those that close completely, hence the phrase 'to clam up'. But it's not quite so simple as that as some clams, such as the razor clam and soft clam, don't shut. The latter is also known as a 'gaper', precisely because it never closes up completely. By contrast, mussels and oysters are bivalve molluscs that close hermetically, but they are never termed clams. Clams are most commonly found in American recipes and, typically, these are venus clams, such as the striped venus. However, for recipes like this, vongole veraci also work perfectly well.

INGREDIENTS

800 g/1 lb 12 oz clams
2 tbsp white wine
4 tbsp fish stock (see page 390)
handful of flat-leaf parsley,
   finely chopped
½ red chilli (chile), deseeded
   and finely chopped
8 cherry tomatoes, quartered
2 garlic cloves, thinly sliced
25 g/1 oz/2 tbsp butter, diced
olive oil
pepper

ALTERNATIVE SHELLFISH

cockles or short-neck (carpet
   shell) clams

Preheat the oven to 180°C/350°F/Gas Mark 4.

Line four soup plates or bowls with sheets of foil and cover each with a sheet of baking parchment (baking paper). Divide the clams, white wine, fish stock, chopped parsley (reserving some for garnish), red chilli (chile), tomatoes and garlic between the parchment sheets. Drizzle over a few drops of olive oil, dot with the diced butter and season lightly with pepper. Arrange the clams on the parchment sheets in a single layer so they are not too tightly packed and their shells have enough room to open as they steam.

Carefully fold the parchment and foil around the clams, sealing the parcels tightly but leaving a space for steam to escape. Place the parcels on a baking sheet and cook in the oven for 10–12 minutes.

Take the parcels out of the oven, open them carefully and check that all the shells have opened. If any haven't, fold the parchment and foil back around the clams and return the parcels briefly to the oven.

To serve, open the parcels and sprinkle the clams with the reserved chopped parsley.

RIF

REYKJAVIK

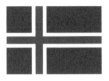

ICELAND

COD, HADDOCK & REDFISH

RIF, ICELAND — 64°55'23.7"N 23°49'14.8"W

FAO 27 ATLANTIC OCEAN NE

FISHERMEN — ÓLI & AARON

40,000 HOOKS
BUT STILL
SUSTAINABLE

It's said the devil went fishing once and he put his hand in the water and grabbed a haddock. You can still see where he held it as there's a black patch on each side of the fish behind the gills – the burn marks where the devil gripped the fish between his thumb and index finger. The haddock struggled and wriggled free from his grip and the two black stripes on both sides are the marks imprinted on it as it escaped.

As cod fisherman Óli Sigmarsson explains, this story was still being told in churches to instil a fear of the devil a hundred years ago. Today, people in those same fishing communities laugh at the tale, but it reveals the profound role fishing has always played in Iceland's society and culture.

Iceland is an extraordinarily beautiful island in the cold north of the Atlantic Ocean. The 'fifties' mint-green moss covering the jet-black lava and the milky blue water of the geothermal springs are colours you won't see elsewhee. The landscape is amazing, too, although not much grows on it amid the glaciers and the volcanoes. Fishing has always been a vital source of food in Iceland and the island's fishery still provides half the country's exports.

The fishing grounds around Iceland are extremely rich. The Icelanders catch pelagic fish such as herring, flatfish and plaice, as well as langoustines, but most of the fish caught are predators such as redfish, haddock and cod. Much of Iceland's cod and haddock is caught by fishermen like Óli. He fishes on a longliner ship, together with around thirteen other crewmen, using a line stretching for miles with as many as 40,000 hooks attached at intervals. Smaller boats also fish with longlines with a crew of just four but their lines may still have as many as 20,000 hooks.

It sounds like an awful lot but Iceland's fishery is sustainable. The government has devised an intricate system of laws that prevents overfishing. It essentially works as follows. Each year, the independent Marine Research Institute assesses the fish stocks and advises the Ministry of Fisheries of its findings. Based on these findings, the minister sets a maximum amount of fish that can be caught and no boat, large or small, is allowed to set out without first having been allocated an individual quota. Each vessel also has to declare all the fish it catches when back on land. Óli's longliner fishes for cod, the fish specified in the skipper's quota, but if it also catches haddock, it still has to bring these in and declare them. The skipper will then exchange part of his cod quota for haddock. An automated national trading system is in place to oversee this, a bit like a stock exchange, which prevents the annual quotas for the different species being exceeded.

The longlines have lead weights attached to them to ensure they sink to the bottom as soon as they are released. This prevents birds and seals becoming entangled in the lines, although crews still worry about the seals, mainly because these picky eaters bite at the bellies of the fish caught on the lines.

In Icelandic waters, by far the most cod is caught by longliners like the one Óli sails. The downside of ensuring an efficient modern fishery is the enormous pressure this places on Iceland's small traditional fishing communities, so in recent years part of the annual quota has been set aside and divided in the summer among the fishing villages along the coast. It means they can still set out in their boats during the day, each with between two and five hand lines and four or five hooks, just as people did generations ago. Iceland's government is therefore able to maintain a sustainable future for both the traditional fishing communities and the fish.

Cod has long been a staple food for Icelanders. One of the oldest ways of preserving it is as stockfish, where it is dried in the air. You can still buy stockfish in Icelandic supermarkets, along with another traditional food that is exclusive to Iceland, *håkarl* – fermented shark. Happily, these days *håkarl* is less readily available because we really shouldn't be eating sharks. The most positive thing that I can say about it is that it tastes like ammonia-flavoured chewing gum, which may explain why it is the traditional accompaniment to extra-strong vodka.

SALAD OF STOCKFISH, APPLE & BEETROOT

STARTER, LUNCH — SERVES 4
PREPARATION 24 HOURS 10 MINUTES — COOKING 15 MINUTES

Drying is an excellent way to cure fish as micro-organisms can't grow without water and so the fish can't rot. In the old days, fish were dried in the open air, which works well in very hot or very cold climates, but in humid, temperate zones like Europe, untreated fish tends to rot before it has dried completely. Centuries ago, people living in temperate climates discovered that drying fish worked if you salted it first and that it also improved its flavour. In Spain, for example, huge quantities of bacalao (salt cod) are still eaten. About one-quarter of the fish is saturated with salt, which prevents harmful bacteria from forming. At the same time, it allows enzymes and salt-resistant bacteria to break down neutral fats and proteins in the flesh into smaller, flavoursome particles that enhance the flavour of the fish even more. It's important to select a piece of fish that is pure white as, if it has a yellowish tinge, it has probably oxidized slightly and won't taste as good. Stockfish, salt-cured cod from northern Europe, is dried even longer (and harder) than bacalao but you can use either for most recipes. Just remember to soak the fish in water for at least 24 hours before cooking.

INGREDIENTS

STOCKFISH & BEETROOT (BEETS)

600 g/1 lb 5 oz stockfish (air and wind-dried white fish, usually cod)
2 beetroot (beets), cooked, peeled and finely diced
100 ml/3½ fl oz/generous ⅓ cup balsamic vinegar

DRESSING

1 tsp Dijon mustard
1 tbsp white wine vinegar
4 tbsp sunflower oil

SALAD

1 small cos (romaine) lettuce, separated into leaves and rinsed
½ Granny Smith apple, cut into matchsticks
½ tbsp finely chopped chives
salt and pepper

ALTERNATIVE FISH

salt cod (bacalao)

Soak the stockfish for 24 hours in a large bowl of cold water, changing the water at least four times.

When you change the water for the final time, begin marinating the beetroot (beets). Place it in a bowl, pour over the balsamic vinegar and leave for 6 hours.

Preheat the oven to 160°C/325°F/Gas Mark 3.

To make the dressing, whisk the mustard and vinegar with a pinch of salt. Add the sunflower oil a few drops at a time, whisking constantly until the dressing thickens. If it is too thick, whisk in a few drops of water. Season with salt and pepper.

Drain the fish from the bowl and pat dry. Put the fish in an ovenproof dish and cook in the oven for 12–15 minutes. Remove any skin and bones and break the fish into pieces. Leave it to cool until lukewarm.

Drain the beetroot from the vinegar and pat dry with kitchen paper (paper towels).

Divide the lettuce leaves between four plates or place on a large serving dish. Arrange the fish, beetroot and apple matchsticks over the leaves and sprinkle with the chives. Drizzle the dressing over the salad or serve it separately.

SMOKED HADDOCK WITH LOVAGE & CELERY REMOULADE

MAIN COURSE — SERVES 4
PREPARATION **10 MINUTES** — COOKING **25 MINUTES**

Smoked haddock is popular in the UK, being eaten all over the British Isles and elsewhere, too. Even the French have adopted it, calling it by its English name, 'haddock'. Smoked haddock began as a Scottish delicacy and several variations can be found, such as Glasgow pales, which are lightly smoked and pale straw in colour. The best known are Arbroath Smokies, where the fish are hot-smoked to turn them a coppery brown colour on the outside with the creamy white flesh inside that has a deliciously savoury flavour.

INGREDIENTS

1 celery stick
600 g/1 lb 5 oz baby new
    potatoes, skins on
handful of lovage leaves, finely
    chopped
100 ml/3½ fl oz/scant ½ cup
    mayonnaise (see page 391)
1 tbsp finely sliced gherkins
1 shallot, finely chopped
splash of lemon juice
splash of Tabasco
4 x 150–175-g/5–6-oz cooked
    smoked haddock fillets
1 slice of rye bread, made into
    crumbs
sunflower oil for baking
salt and pepper

ALTERNATIVE FISH

hot smoked salmon

Preheat the oven to 150°C/300°F/Gas Mark 2. Prepare a bowl of iced water.

Trim the base from the celery stick, pull off any tough strings and dice.

Bring a large pan of water to the boil and blanch the celery for 1–2 minutes. Lift the celery out of the water with a draining spoon and transfer to the bowl of iced water.

Add the potatoes to the hot water in the pan and boil for 6–8 minutes until they are almost tender but still give some resistance when pierced with the tip of a knife. Drain and leave to cool.

To make the remoulade, drain the celery and set aside 2 tablespoons of the chopped lovage. Mix the mayonnaise with the celery, gherkins, shallot and remaining lovage. Season with lemon juice, Tabasco, salt and pepper and set aside.

Line a baking sheet with baking parchment (baking paper), place the haddock on it and put in the oven for 5–7 minutes. This is only to heat the fish. After all, the fish is already cooked and smoked.

Heat 6 tablespoons of sunflower oil in a frying pan (skillet) over a high heat. Fry the baby potatoes for 8–10 minutes until golden brown, turning regularly. Add the reserved lovage leaves 30 seconds before the potatoes are ready. Remove from the pan and season the potatoes with salt.

Take the haddock out of the oven. Serve the fish with a spoonful of the remoulade alongside and the potatoes. Sprinkle the rye breadcrumbs over the fish.

PINTO BEANS
WITH COD & THYME

MAIN COURSE – SERVES 4
PREPARATION 12 HOURS – COOKING 1 HOUR 15 MINUTES

As with meat I love fish on the bone. Why? Because the bones give a lot of flavour to the dish that wouldn't ordinarily be there if cooked filleted. We should learn that there is a good reason to use the whole of the fish and cut pieces straight through the bone. You benefit from extra flavour and it is less expensive because there is no waste.

INGREDIENTS

300 g/10 oz dried pinto beans
1 carrot, thinly sliced
1 onion, coarsely chopped
1 celery stick, finely chopped
2 bay leaves
10 sprigs of thyme, leaves
   stripped from their stalks
25 g/1 oz/2 tbsp butter
2 tbsp plain (all-purpose) flour
2 tbsp sherry vinegar
4 x 160–180-g/5½–6½-oz cod
   steaks
extra virgin olive oil
groundnut (peanut) oil, for
   frying
salt and pepper

ALTERNATIVE FISH

haddock or hake

Soak the pinto beans in a large bowl of cold water for 12 hours.

Drain and rinse the beans by running cold water over them. Heat 2 tablespoons of extra virgin olive oil in a deep pan over a medium-high heat and sauté the carrot, onion and celery for 2 minutes until translucent. Pour in 1 litre/1¼ pints/4¼ cups of cold water, add the bay leaves, thyme – reserving a few thyme leaves for garnish – and the beans. Simmer, stirring occasionally, for 40–50 minutes or until the beans are tender but still have some 'bite'. Drain the beans, reserving the cooking liquid, and season to taste with salt and pepper. Cover the beans to keep them warm.

Melt the butter in a saucepan. Remove from the heat and stir in the flour until smooth. Cook over a low heat for 1–2 minutes. Add 200 ml/7 fl oz/scant 1 cup of the bean cooking liquid and stir or whisk until the sauce is thickened and smooth. Stir in the beans and sherry vinegar and season with salt and pepper.

Heat some groundnut (peanut) oil for shallow frying in a frying pan (skillet) over a high heat and fry the cod until lightly browned on both sides. This will take 4–5 minutes, depending on the thickness of the steaks.

Spoon the pinto beans into deep serving plates and lift the cod steaks on top. Garnish with the reserved thyme leaves.

FRIED REDFISH FILLET WITH CRISPY SKIN & QUINOA SALAD

LUNCH, MAIN COURSE — SERVES 4
PREPARATION 10 MINUTES — COOKING 25 MINUTES

Fried fish is perfect for a quick, healthy meal at lunch or dinner. It comes together quickly with simply prepared ancient grains such quinoa which can be cooked in minutes.

INGREDIENTS

250 g/9 oz white quinoa
2 tbsp pumpkin seeds
finely grated zest and juice of
  1 orange
1 tsp Dijon mustard
1 tbsp white wine vinegar
4 tbsp extra virgin olive oil
4 tbsp pomegranate seeds
handful of mint leaves roughly
  chopped
½ red onion, roughly chopped
  or finely sliced
handful of rocket (arugula)
  leaves, roughly chopped
4 x 150–175-g/5–6-oz redfish
  fillets, skin on
groundnut (peanut) oil for frying
salt and pepper

Put the quinoa in a fine sieve (strainer) and rinse by running cold running water over it. Tip the quinoa into a small saucepan and add 500 ml/18 fl oz/2 cups of cold water plus a pinch of salt. Bring to the boil, reduce the heat to low and simmer for 15 minutes, stirring occasionally, until all the liquid has been absorbed. Set aside to cool.

Roast the pumpkin seeds in a dry frying pan (skillet) over a medium-high heat for 1 minute.

In a large bowl, whisk together the orange zest, juice, mustard, white wine vinegar and olive oil with a fork and season with salt and pepper. Stir in the quinoa. Reserve some of the pomegranate seeds, pumpkin seeds and chopped mint for garnish and stir the rest into the quinoa with the red onion and rocket (arugula) leaves.

Using a sharp knife, cut diagonal slashes in the skin of the redfish fillets at 2-cm/¾-inch intervals. Season with salt and pepper and brush the fillets all over with groundnut (peanut) oil. Heat a frying pan (skillet) over a high heat, add the fish, skin-side down, and, lowering the heat to medium-high, fry without moving the fillets around for 3–5 minutes, depending on their thickness. Turn the fillets over and fry for a further 2–3 minutes but don't turn them again or their skin will lose its crispness.

Serve the quinoa salad with the fish fillets, garnished with the reserved pomegranate seeds, pumpkin seeds and mint.

COD CONFIT IN OLIVE OIL

MAIN COURSE — SERVES 4
COOKING 30 MINUTES

While fried fish is delicious, another excellent way to cook it is as a 'confit'. To confit, means to cook meat or fish slowly in a large quantity of fat at low temperature (usually around 60°C/140°F for fish). This cooking method was originally devised as a way of preserving meat, as by covering it in a thick, airtight layer of fat, the cooked meat could be kept for a long time. It had to be well salted, as although the low cooking temperature meant the meat was pasteurized, it wasn't sterilized. Today we no longer have to add extra salt and we confit food more as an alternative way of cooking than to preserve it. It is similar to sous vide cooking but doesn't require any special equipment. Sous vide is a technique frequently used in chic restaurants and involves putting the food in vacuum-sealed bags and cooking it at a low temperature in a water bath. The advantage of preparing fish as a confit is that it is completely covered in oil and doesn't dry out, resulting in a very succulent and juicy piece of cod. And you can reuse the oil for other fish dishes.

INGREDIENTS

1 litre/1 ¾ pints/4¼ cups light olive oil for frying*
1 onion, sliced
½ bulb of garlic, cut in half
½ fennel bulb, sliced
1 red chilli (chile), cut in half lengthwise just below the stalk
2 bay leaves
4 sprigs of thyme
2 sprigs of rosemary
½ lemon, sliced
4 x 150-g/5-oz cod fillets, skinned
400 g/14 oz baby new potatoes, skins on
25 g/1 oz/2 tbsp butter
handful of flat-leaf parsley, finely chopped

*use light olive oil not extra virgin olive oil for frying

ALTERNATIVE FISH

haddock, pollock or hake

Heat 1 tablespoon of the olive oil in a large, deep saucepan over a low heat and sauté the onion, garlic, fennel and chilli (chile) for 2 minutes without allowing them to brown. Add the bay leaves, thyme, rosemary and lemon slices and then pour in the rest of the oil.

Stand a cooking thermometer in the pan and heat the oil until it reaches 60°C/140°F. Lower the cod fillets carefully into the oil, adding more oil if the fish is not completely covered. Fry the fish for about 15 minutes, making sure the temperature of the oil stays around 60°C/140°F.

Put the potatoes in a saucepan of lightly salted water and bring to the boil. Cook for 10–15 minutes until tender and then drain and add the butter and parsley. Mix well and keep warm with a lid on the pan.

Drain the cod. Serve it with the onion and herbs and some of the aromatic oil from the pan. Accompany with the potatoes.

FISH FINGERS & KETCHUP

CANAPÉ, STARTER, LUNCH – SERVES 4
PREPARATION **10 MINUTES** – COOKING **20 MINUTES**

Johannes van Dam was without doubt the Netherlands' leading food writer of the twentieth century. He owned the biggest library of cookbooks in Europe (perhaps even the world), which is now housed in the University of Amsterdam. I got to know van Dam when he started buying fish at my first shop and he became my mentor. Each time I was planning a new book, I would start by talking to Johannes, as a chat with him was worth four years at hotel school. Johannes was a friendly man but, if he spotted you making a mistake, he was merciless. We were once invited to do a blind fish finger tasting on television and a camping stove was set up in the studio to fry them on. "You can't fry fish fingers on that," Johannes protested and he certainly didn't mince his words. That day we got a two-hour lecture on fish fingers, from the right type of fish and the fillet being in one piece, not scraps pressed together, to the correct proportion of fish to crust and that the crust shouldn't have too much flavour as it would detract from the fish. I now know everything there is to know about fish fingers!

ICELAND – COD, HADDOCK & REDFISH

INGREDIENTS

KETCHUP

1 red onion, chopped
2 garlic cloves, finely chopped
1 tbsp tomato purée (paste)
1 x 400-g (14½-oz) can of plum
   tomatoes
2 tbsp brown sugar
2 tbsp red wine vinegar
Tabasco

FISH FINGERS

600 g/1 lb 5oz cod steak, in one
   piece, skinned
100 g/4 oz/1 cup panko (or dry
   breadcrumbs)
2 tbsp paprika
50 g/2 oz/scant ½ cup plain
   (all-purpose) flour
2 eggs, beaten
oil, for frying
salt and pepper

ALTERNATIVE FISH

pollock or hake

To make the ketchup, heat 2 tablespoons of oil in a frying pan (skillet) over a medium-high heat and fry the onion until softened, but not browned. Add the garlic and fry for another 2 minutes, stirring frequently. Add the tomato purée (paste) and stir over the heat for a further 2 minutes. Add the plum tomatoes and their juice, stir well and crush the tomatoes lightly with the back of the spoon. Cook for 5 minutes over a low heat, add the sugar, vinegar, a few drops of Tabasco and a pinch of salt, and leave until the sauce reduces by two-thirds. Push the sauce through a metal sieve (strainer) to make it smooth. Taste and season with salt and pepper. Cool, transfer to a bowl, cover and chill in the refrigerator until needed.

Cut the cod fillets into fish finger shapes. You can make them any size but they all need to be approximately the same thickness so they cook in the same length of time. Pat the fish fingers dry with kitchen paper (paper towels) and season with salt and pepper. Mix the panko with the paprika, coat the fish in the flour, then in beaten egg and finally in the panko-paprika mix. Set aside.

Heat 300 ml/10 fl oz/1¼ cups of oil in a frying pan over a high heat. The oil should be heated to a temperature of 180°C/350°F and reach roughly halfway up the fish fingers when you add them to the pan. You can check the oil is the correct temperature by using a thermometer or by adding a small piece of white bread, which should rise immediately to the surface of the oil and brown quickly.

Fry the fish fingers for 3–4 minutes on each side until golden brown. Remove from the pan and drain on kitchen paper.

Serve the fish fingers with the ketchup.

REDFISH
BAKED IN THE OVEN

MAIN COURSE — SERVES 4
PREPARATION **10 MINUTES** — COOKING **35 MINUTES**

There is a hotel in the northwest of Iceland called Hotel Budir. It is one of the most remote hotels I have ever visited and has its own fishing dock. The story goes that the owner of the hotel always asks you if you have a dream upon arrival – you can only stay if you have a dream. We stopped here for the night and made this redfish in the hotel kitchen. It tasted like a dream.

INGREDIENTS

1 large redfish weighing about
  1–1.5 kg/2 lb 4 oz–3 lb 5 oz
  (or 4 small fish weighing
  about 300–350 g/10–12 oz
  each), cleaned
4 garlic cloves, skin left on and
  bruised
4 sprigs of thyme (8 small sprigs
  if using individual fish)
2 sprigs of rosemary (8 small
  sprigs if using individual fish)
½ lime, sliced
splash of lime juice
extra virgin olive oil
salt and pepper

ALTERNATIVE FISH

sea bass or sea bream

Preheat the oven to 180°C/350°F/Gas Mark 4.

Cut finger-length slashes at 2-cm/¾-inch intervals in the skin on both sides of the redfish. Mix half of the garlic, thyme and rosemary with 4 tablespoons of olive oil in a bowl and set aside for 5 minutes to infuse. Season the inside of the fish with salt and pepper. Remove the garlic and herbs from the oil and tuck into the cavity. Add the lime slices and spoon in a little of the infused olive oil.

Brush olive oil over the outside of the fish and into the slashes in the skin. Season again. Grease a large baking sheet with olive oil and lift the fish into it. Finely chop the remaining thyme and rosemary and scatter over the fish. Tuck the remaining garlic cloves over and around the fish.

Bake a large fish in the oven for 30–35 minutes, or 20–30 minutes for smaller fish. To check the fish is cooked, press a spoon into the middle of the flesh and if the flesh comes away easily from the backbone, it is ready.

Serve the fish drizzled with a little extra olive oil and a splash of lime. Grind over some salt and pepper.

COD CEVICHE

STARTER, LUNCH — SERVES 4
PREPARATION **20 MINUTES**

Ceviche is a wonderfully fresh fish dish from Latin America. Essentially, it's pieces of raw fish in a citrus marinade, the acidity in the marinade producing a similar effect as cooking with heat. The citrus juice causes proteins in the fish to solidify, making the flesh appear opaque and firmer, although not as firm as if it had been cooked, and it also changes the flavour less. It was Martin Morales, the British-Peruvian chef at Ceviche restaurant in London, who taught me how to prepare ceviche. Martin is typical of the new generation of chefs, so naturally his food is all about eating well, but he also sees gastronomy as part of a much greater, artistic world. Martin is a DJ too, and exhibits Peruvian art in his restaurant. He's concerned about the future and only works with sustainable ingredients, even though these are not always easy to come by, such as Peruvian amarillo peppers, which Martin always uses in his ceviche marinade. Other peppers are fine, as long as the marinade is nice and spicy. In Peru they call this marinade 'tiger's milk' and sometimes they drink it with a shot of pisco (Peruvian liqueur), when it becomes 'panther's milk'. It's reputed to make men more potent.

INGREDIENTS

1/2 red onion, thinly sliced

1 tomato, quartered, deseeded and thinly sliced

1 chilli (chile), deseeded and thinly sliced

4 limes

1-cm/1/2-inch piece of fresh root ginger, peeled

1 garlic clove, peeled and left whole

4 sprigs of coriander (cilantro), leaves pulled off the stalks and both leaves and stalks reserved

1/2 tsp amarillo paste (or another yellow chilli paste)

2 tsp fish stock

1 tsp evaporated milk

about 300 g/10 oz cod fillet, skinned

1 avocado, peeled, pitted and diced

1/2 sweet potato, peeled, boiled and diced

2 tbsp pomegranate seeds

salt

ALTERNATIVE FISH

salmon, haddock or redfish

Mix the red onion, tomato and chilli (chile) slices together in a bowl. In Peru, they often slice onions from top to bottom instead of 'across the equator'. Put the bowl in the freezer to make the slices nice and crisp.

Squeeze the juice of 3 limes into a large bowl and add the ginger, garlic and coriander (cilantro) stalks to the juice. Set aside for 5–10 minutes so the flavours have time to develop. Remove the ginger, garlic and coriander and add 1/4 teaspoon of salt and the amarillo paste to the bowl. Stir in the fish stock and evaporated milk (don't use fresh milk or it may curdle) to make the tiger's milk marinade less acidic, and mix well. Add the fish and leave to marinate for 5 minutes, stirring occasionally. Mix in the avocado and sweet potato.

Take the bowl containing the onion, tomato and chilli out of the freezer and squeeze in the juice from the remaining lime. Mix in the coriander leaves and season to taste with salt.

Serve the ceviche in a dish or on a plate. Sprinkle the pomegranate seeds over the top and then the tomato, onion and chilli salad.

BRANDADE OF HADDOCK & SMOKED TROUT

MAIN COURSE — SERVES 4
PREPARATION **1 HOUR** — COOKING **1 HOUR 10 MINUTES**

A classic brandade from the south of France doesn't contain any potato. The original brandade de morue Nîmoise consisted of salt cod beaten with milk and olive oil until it had the consistency of mashed potato. In the city of Nîmes, where brandade is a speciality, they never even added garlic, although this is allowed in Marseille and Toulon. But away from southern France, brandade has long been made with mashed potato, maybe to save money or perhaps because people prefer it that way. Whatever the reason, it's become the norm these days and brandade is hardly ever made without the addition of mashed potato. This recipe does contain potato but, instead of salt cold, we've used fresh haddock and a bit of smoked trout. We've also added Asian spices simply for their flavour, but keep quiet about that in Nîmes!

INGREDIENTS

400 g/14 oz haddock fillet, skinned
500 g/1 lb 2 oz floury potatoes, peeled and cut into even-size chunks
500 ml/18 fl oz/2 cups milk
2 stalks of lemongrass, crushed and roughly chopped
2 bay leaves
4 sprigs of thyme
2 garlic cloves, crushed
1 shallot, roughly chopped
1 red chilli (chile), thinly sliced
50g/2 oz/4 tbsp butter, diced
2 tbsp chopped coriander (cilantro) leaves
100 g/4 oz smoked trout fillet, broken into small pieces
3 tbsp dry breadcrumbs
salt and pepper

ALTERNATIVE FISH

cod, pollock or hake

Season the haddock on both sides with salt and pepper. Chill the fish in the refrigerator for 1 hour.

Put the potatoes in a pan of lightly salted water and bring to the boil. Cook for 15–20 minutes until the potatoes are tender. Drain and leave them to steam dry without covering the pan.

Meanwhile, heat the milk in a saucepan over a low heat. Add the lemongrass, bay leaves, thyme, garlic, shallot and chilli (chile). Turn the heat down as low as possible and leave the mixture to infuse for 30 minutes. Strain the milk, return it to the pan and reheat on low. Add the haddock and poach in the milk for 12–15 minutes, depending on the thickness of the fillet, until cooked. Preheat the grill (broiler). Lift the fish out of the pan with a draining spoon, reserving the milk, and flake the flesh into small pieces.

Add the butter and 100 ml/3½ fl oz/generous ⅓ cup of the hot milk to the potatoes. Mash and season with salt and pepper.

Reserve some of the coriander (cilantro) and trout for garnish and stir the rest, with the haddock, through the mashed potatoes. Spoon the mixture into a heatproof dish and arrange the reserved coriander and trout over the top. Sprinkle with the breadcrumbs and grill (broil) for 4–6 minutes, until golden brown.

HADDOCK FILLET WITH SEA VEGETABLES & ALMONDS

MAIN COURSE — SERVES 4
PREPARATION 10 MINUTES — COOKING 15 MINUTES

Marsh samphire (sea asparagus/sea beans) is a sea vegetable that grows on the shore and in dunes, marshes and mudflats. Seawater regularly washes over it and, when the tide is in, it is underwater which gives it a briny flavour. While it used to be harvested in the wild, some farmers have been so successful at creating a coastal environment that samphire can now be cultivated. Marsh samphire should be eaten relatively young, while the shiny deep-green stalks are firm and strong, as later in the season they get tougher and less appetizing. At one time it was best not to buy wild marsh samphire after the end of July but now that it is being cultivated, young samphire is available all year round. It's a lovely vegetable with a briny flavour that combines beautifully with fish. Take care when preparing it, though, as, the more you rinse samphire, the less briny it will taste.

INGREDIENTS

50 g/2 oz/4 tbsp butter
2 tbsp whole almonds, blanched but not toasted
4 x 150-g/5-oz haddock fillets, skinned
plain (all-purpose) flour
125 g/4½ oz marsh samphire (sea asparagus/sea beans)
75 g/3 oz sea lavender
1 garlic clove, peeled and left whole
12 caperberries
finely grated of zest ½ lemon
groundnut (peanut) oil
salt and white pepper

ALTERNATIVE FISH

cod, pollock or hake

Heat 10 g/½ oz/1 tablespoon of the butter in a frying pan (skillet) over a medium-high heat. Add the almonds and fry until they are golden brown. Drain the almonds from the pan and set aside. Wipe out the pan with kitchen paper (paper towels).

Pat the fish dry with kitchen paper and season with salt and white pepper. Coat the fish all over in flour, brushing off any excess. Heat 4 tablespoons of groundnut (peanut) oil in a frying pan over a high heat and brown the fish on both sides for 3–4 minutes, depending on the thickness of the fillets. Lower the heat, add 20 g/¾ oz/1½ tablespoons of the butter and, when it has melted, tilt the pan and baste the butter several times over the fish with a spoon. Drain the fish from the pan with a spatula and cover the fillets with foil to keep them warm or place in the oven on its lowest setting.

Melt the remaining butter in a clean frying pan and add the marsh samphire (sea asparagus/sea beans) and sea lavender. Skewer the garlic clove on the prongs of a fork and stir it around in the pan for 1–2 minutes until the vegetables are translucent. Add the caperberries and almonds and season with a little pepper. It's not necessary to add salt as the sea vegetables are sufficiently salty already.

Divide the vegetables between four serving plates. Scatter over the lemon zest and drizzle with some of the buttery juices from the pan. Top with the fish fillets and serve.

COD WITH PARMA HAM & SAGE

MAIN COURSE — SERVES 4
PREPARATION 5 MINUTES — COOKING 25 MINUTES

This unwrapped version of the traditionally wrapped cod is perhaps the quickest dish to make in this book. It is inspired by the Italians who wrap a piece of fish in a slice of ham with sage tucked inside and pan-fry it with olive oil. The combination of the salty ham with the flavour of the sage and the fine texture of the white fish is fantastic.

INGREDIENTS

100 g/4 oz Parma ham slices, or
    another cured ham such as
    Serrano
4 x 150–175-g/5–6-oz cod
    fillets, skinned
handful of sage leaves
extra virgin olive oil
salt and pepper

ALTERNATIVE FISH

haddock or hake

Preheat the oven to 180°C/350°F/Gas Mark 4.

Lay the slices of ham on a rack and roast in the oven for 8–10 minutes until crisp. Transfer the ham to a plate lined with kitchen paper (paper towels) and leave to cool.

Season the cod with salt and pepper but avoid using too much salt as the ham is already quite salty. Grease an ovenproof dish with olive oil and lay the cod in it. Drizzle with olive oil and add the sage leaves, turning them over so they are coated in oil, to prevent them burning. Roast the cod in the oven for 12–15 minutes, depending on the thickness of the fillets.

Serve the cod straight from the dish topped with the crisp Parma ham.

BACALAO (SALT COD) CROQUETTES WITH REMOULADE SAUCE

CANAPÉ, STARTER — SERVES 4
PREPARATION 26 HOURS 15 MINUTES — COOKING 30 MINUTES

Make sure you soak the salted cod for a good amount of time (at least 24 hours). I recommend cold water below but you could also use milk, which will remove some of the added saltiness. Be patient with the soaking if you don't want the croquettes to taste overly satly. This is something you might like to make ahead of time, the day before a party.

INGREDIENTS

400 g/14 oz bacalao (salt cod)
400 g/14 oz potatoes, peeled and cut into even-size chunks
450 ml/15 fl oz/1 3/4 cups milk
25 g/1 oz/2 tbsp butter, diced
1 bay leaf
8 peppercorns
handful of chives, finely chopped
handful of curly-leaf parsley, finely chopped, plus extra sprigs to garnish
handful of coriander (cilantro) leaves, finely chopped
1 tsp smoked paprika
100 g/4 oz/3/4 cup plain (all-purpose) flour, spread out on a plate
2 eggs, beaten in a shallow dish
100 g/4 oz/1 cup breadcrumbs, spread out on a plate
groundnut (peanut) oil, for deep-frying
salt and pepper
1 lemon, cut into wedges , to serve

REMOULADE SAUCE

100 g/4 oz/scant 1/2 cup mayonnaise
2 tbsp finely sliced gherkins
1 tbsp finely chopped capers
1 shallot, chopped
1 tbsp finely chopped chives
1 tbsp finely chopped curly-leaf parsley
Worcestershire sauce

Soak the bacalao (salt cod) for 24 hours in a large bowl of cold water, changing the water four times at regular intervals.

Put the potatoes in a pan of lightly salted water, bring to the boil and cook for 15–20 minutes or until tender. Drain, let the potatoes dry in the steam and then mash them with 3 tablespoons of the milk and the butter.

Pour the remaining milk into a pan, add the fish, bay leaf and peppercorns, and poach for 5–7 minutes or until the fish is cooked. Drain the fish from the pan, leave to cool and then discard the skin and any bones. Flake the fish and add to the mashed potato with the chives, parsley, coriander (cilantro) and paprika. Stir everything together until evenly combined and then chill in the refrigerator for 2 hours.

Shape the potato mixture into croquettes with your hands. Coat in flour, brush with beaten egg and then roll in breadcrumbs until evenly coated.

To make the remoulade sauce, stir together the mayonnaise, gherkins, capers, shallot, chives and parsley until evenly combined. Season with Worcestershire sauce, salt and pepper.

Heat groundnut (peanut) oil in a deep-fat fryer or tall, heavy-based saucepan to 180°C/350°F.

Deep-fry the croquettes in batches for about 5 minutes until golden brown and then drain on kitchen paper (paper towels). When all the croquettes have been cooked, deep-fry sprigs of parsley for a few seconds until crisp. Drain well on kitchen paper.

Serve the croquettes with the remoulade sauce, garnished with the fried parsley sprigs and lemon wedges.

FRIED WHITING WITH PARSNIPS

MAIN COURSE — SERVES 4
PREPARATION 10 MINUTES — COOKING 15 MINUTES

The whiting caught in Icelandic waters is currently being assessed for the right to display the MSC ecolabel. Whiting is a fairly small member of the cod family but its flavour is equally good.

INGREDIENTS

4 parsnips, peeled
4 x 150–175-g/5–6-oz whiting
  fillets, skin on
50 g/2 oz/4 tbsp clarified butter
  (see page 392)
200 g/7 oz mixed green salad
  leaves
2 tbsp walnut oil
1 tbsp chopped hazelnuts
groundnut (peanut) oil, for
  deep-frying and brushing
salt and pepper

ALTERNATIVE FISH

red mullet or gurnard

Heat groundnut (peanut) oil in a deep-fat fryer or tall, heavy-based saucepan to 180°C/350°F. Check the temperature of the oil with a cooking thermometer or by adding a cube of white bread, which should immediately rise to the surface and start to brown.

While the oil is heating up, shave the parsnips into long thin strips using a vegetable peeler or mandoline. Add the strips to the hot oil and deep-fry until golden brown. Drain onto a plate lined with kitchen paper (paper towels) and sprinkle with salt.

Pat the whiting fillets dry with kitchen paper. Brush groundnut oil over the fillets and season with salt and pepper. Heat a dry frying pan (skillet) over a high heat and lay the fillets in it skin-side down. Fry without moving the fish around so the skin becomes crisp. When the flesh turns white and is no longer translucent – after about 3–4 minutes – turn the fillets over carefully with a spatula. Fry for 1–2 minutes, depending on the thickness of the fillets, until cooked.

Drain the fish onto a plate lined with kitchen paper. Add the clarified butter to the pan. Stir until the butter melts and turns a rich golden brown and has the aroma of roasted nuts – known as 'beurre noisette'.

Dress the salad leaves with the walnut oil and mix in the chopped hazelnuts.

Serve the fish, skin-side up, with the 'beurre noisette' drizzled over and around. Accompany with the parsnip 'crisps' ('chips') and salad.

NEWLYN

LONDON

UNITED KINGDOM

HAKE, SARDINES & MACKEREL

NEWLYN. ENGLAND — 50°06'25.4"N 5°33'01.2"W

FAO 27 ATLANTIC OCEAN NE

FISHERMEN — ALAN & DAVID

EVERYONE LOVES SARDINES IN CORNWALL

How to define 'quaint'? It's such a typically English word and impossible to translate into another language. It means something is picturesque and charming, in an old-fashioned, low-key way – a little peculiar, but in a nice way. An old house might be quaint, or a whole village, like the fishing port of Newlyn on the Cornish coast. At the southwestern tip of the United Kingdom, it faces directly out into the Atlantic Ocean.

Newlyn is a small place with old houses built against the cliffs. It's a little bit drab but rather homely too – quaint, in fact. On a clear day you can see across the bay to the small island of St Michael's Mount, with its castle and church, the oldest building on the island, dating from the twelfth century. When the tide is out you can walk across to it.

Boats enter the harbour all night long. Those that fish during the day with ring nets, or bottom trawlers, return as soon as their holds are full, which could be before midnight or at three o'clock in the morning. Larger boats bringing in hake dock several times a week. Their catch is brought ashore, sorted by type into red crates filled with ice, before being placed in a large shed near the quay, separated out according to the boat that landed it. The auction begins at six o'clock sharp in the morning. It's an old-fashioned, well-mannered affair with an auctioneer selling the crates to a throng of around twenty dealers. Gradually he nudges up the price: two twenty, two thirty, two forty and so on. The price is per kilo and buyers state how many crates they want at that price and place a card with their firm's name on the crates. There's no technology involved, the auctioneer writes everything down on his notepad with a pencil.

There are all sorts of fish in the red crates – pollock, gurnard, turbot, cod, octopus, bib (pout), sunfish and lots of hake – and these days there are plenty of sardines at the Newlyn fish auction as well. Cornwall's sardine fishery has a long and interesting history as, at one time, canned sardines were widely eaten in the south of England. They were better known in Britain as pilchards but they went out of fashion several decades ago when they acquired the reputation of being what Grandma ate or what you fed to the cat. The British wanted more upmarket fish or, of course, fish and chips. It was not until the early noughties when one smart Brit saw those same sardines on a barbecue across the Channel in Brittany and suggested reinventing pilchards as Cornish sardines. Suddenly the British loved them again!

Cornish sardines are exactly the same as Breton sardines since they come from the same robust Atlantic stock. The British fish for them in small boats using ring nets so all Cornish sardines are MSC-certified. The same applies to the majority of the hake as in Cornwall it is caught by no more than fifteen boats that fish exclusively for it. Any uncertified hake is bycatch brought in by bottom trawlers.

One of those fifteen boats is the *Ajax*, captained by skipper Alan Dwan. Originally from Ireland, as is evident as soon as he starts to speak, he used to fish salmon but Atlantic salmon had been almost wiped out. At one point Alan was permitted to fish salmon for only four weeks a year, which was barely worth his while. He found he was catching more hake in his nets so he cast his salmon nets a little deeper and switched to hake. Twelve years ago, he moved to Cornwall as the sandbanks along Mount's Bay between Lizard Point and Gwennap Head are full of hake.

Hake is fished with vertical nets that rest on the bottom. Alan's boat has six nets, each two miles long, and casting them out takes a full fifteen minutes. The bottom of each net is weighted with lead and the top held up with floats, so the net stays upright all night. Alan and his crew of five often stay at sea for five days at a time. It's a large boat, the nets take up a lot of room and cleaning and chilling the fish also requires space, so they all sleep in one cabin, in bunks with sleeping bags and a small curtain. No one minds the snoring, says Alan, as you can't hear it above the noise of the engine anyway.

These are good times for Alan and his crew. Hake is plentiful and is growing in popularity due to its excellent flavour. For example, British fish and chip shops are increasingly offering hake and there are already fifty fish and chip shops in the United Kingdom with MSC certification.

HAKE STEAKS
WITH ROASTED PEPPERS

MAIN COURSE — SERVES 4
PREPARATION 5 MINUTES — COOKING 30 MINUTES

One way to ensure a balanced consumption of seafood is to try different species and hake is a brilliant substitute for fish like cod and haddock. We did a blind taste test on 'Jamie and Jimmy's Friday Night Food Fight' and the diners couldn't tell the difference.

INGREDIENTS

4 (bell) peppers (2 orange and
  2 yellow), deseeded and cut
  into thick wedges
4 x 175–200-g/6–7-oz hake
  steaks
2 tbsp plain (all-purpose) flour
I tbsp capers
4 sprigs of flat-leaf parsley,
  finely chopped
finely grated zest and juice of
  I lemon
I lemon, cut into wedges
extra virgin olive oil
groundnut (peanut) oil, for
  frying
salt and pepper

ALTERNATIVE FISH

cod or salmon steaks

Preheat the oven to 220°C/425°F/Gas Mark 7.

Brush the (bell) peppers all over with olive oil and season with salt and pepper. Line a baking sheet with baking parchment (baking paper) and place the peppers on it, skin-side up. Roast in the oven for 15–20 minutes until the peppers have softened. Leave to cool and then carefully remove the skins with the tip of a knife. Drizzle the peppers with olive oil and season with salt and pepper.

Pat the fish dry with kitchen paper (paper towels). Roll the steaks in the flour until coated on both sides, brushing off any excess. Season all over with salt and pepper.

Heat the groundnut (peanut) oil in a frying pan (skillet) over a high heat. Add the hake and fry on one side for 3–4 minutes, shaking the pan to stop the steaks sticking to it. Turn them over with a spatula, taking care not to break their delicate flesh.

Add a few dashes of olive oil, the roasted peppers and the capers to the pan and fry for 3 minutes. Test whether the fish is cooked by pressing gently on the flesh and if it comes away from the bone easily, it is done.

Transfer the fish and peppers to a serving dish. Add the parsley, half the lemon zest and a few drops of the juice to the cooking liquid in the pan and pour over the hake. Sprinkle with the remaining lemon zest, season with pepper and serve with lemon wedges to squeeze over.

FISH STEW OF HAKE WITH MARSH SAMPHIRE (SEA ASPARAGUS/SEA BEANS)

MAIN COURSE – SERVES 4
PREPARATION 1 HOUR 5 MINUTES – COOKING 20 MINUTES

Television cooking programmes used to be dull and boring, invariably filmed in a bare studio and purely instructional in content. While travelling along the Cornish coast, I was reminded of the man who first inspired me, Keith Floyd. He was a great English chef of the 1980s, who totally transformed cooking on television. He was the first to cook on location, either on a boat or in the middle of a vineyard, but that wasn't the only reason his shows were so popular. Floyd was a flamboyant character who always wore a bow tie and had a full glass of wine to hand. He made cooking on television fun to watch, even if you weren't planning on cooking yourself, and his shows were chaotic and exciting. If things went wrong, they went wrong, it was as simple as that – and on the BBC at prime time. Whenever I find myself standing in the mud with a cooker on a pile of wooden pallets, I think of Keith Floyd, who invented the whole idea.

INGREDIENTS

600 g/1 lb 5 oz hake fillet, skinned and cut into 4 equal-size pieces
coarse sea salt
1 onion, sliced
2 celery sticks, roughly chopped
1 fennel bulb, sliced
1 carrot, sliced
1 garlic clove, finely chopped
2 bay leaves
small handful of thyme sprigs
handful of flat-leaf parsley, stalks and leaves separated and chopped
zest of 4 oranges, removed in strips with a vegetable peeler
600 ml/1 pint/2½ cups of fish stock (see page 390), or enough to cover the fish
150 g/5 oz baby new potatoes, peeled
100 g/4 oz marsh samphire (sea asparagus/sea beans)
groundnut (peanut) oil
salt and pepper

ALTERNATIVE FISH

cod or haddock

Place the pieces of hake in a dish. Cover with a layer of coarse sea salt and chill in the refrigerator for 1 hour.

Transfer the hake from the dish to a colander and run cold water over it for 5 minutes to ensure all the salt is rinsed off. The fish will have become firmer in texture, lighter in colour and opaque.

Heat 1 tablespoon of groundnut (peanut) oil in a pan, add the onion, celery, fennel, carrot and garlic and fry for 3 minutes without colouring. Add the bay leaves, thyme, parsley stalks and orange zest. Stir for 1 minute and then pour in the stock. Add the potatoes and bring to the boil.

Lower the heat and simmer for 8 minutes. Add the fish and simmer for a further 5 minutes before adding the marsh samphire (sea asparagus/sea beans) and chopped parsley leaves. Cook for a further 1 minute. Taste and season with salt and pepper – salt may not be needed as the marsh samphire is already quite salty.

The fish stew is excellent served with aioli (see page 253).

FISH & CHIPS
WITH HAKE FILLET

LUNCH, MAIN COURSE — SERVES 4
PREPARATION **35 MINUTES** — COOKING **20 MINUTES**

Today's fish and chips are a relatively recent invention. In Oliver Twist, published in 1839, Charles Dickens writes about a shop selling fried fish, but in those days the fish would have been served with a chunk of bread. The combination of battered fried fish, served with chips (fries), dates from the 1860s and has grown in popularity becoming the UK's national dish. During those 150 years the recipe has changed very little.

INGREDIENTS

BEER BATTER

160 g/5½ oz/1½ cup plain
   (all-purpose) flour, sifted
1 tsp baking powder
200 ml/7 fl oz/scant 1 cup
   chilled beer
salt

TARTARE SAUCE

150 ml/5 fl oz/⅔ cup
   mayonnaise
1 shallot, finely sliced
1 tbsp capers
2 tbsp gherkins, finely sliced
6 chives, finely chopped
4 sprigs of flat-leaf parsley,
   finely chopped
1 egg, hard-boiled (hard-
   cooked) and peeled
Tabasco

MUSHY PEAS

20 g/¾ oz/1½ tbsp butter
250 g/9 oz green or marrowfat
   peas (cooked weight)
10 sprigs of mint, leaves only

FISH & CHIPS

800 g/1 lb 12 oz floury potatoes,
   cut into chips (fries)
1 litre/1 ¾ pints/4¼ cups
   groundnut (peanut) oil for
   deep-frying
4 x 150-175-g/5-6-oz hake
   fillets, skinned
plain (all-purpose) flour, for
   dusting
2 lemons, cut into wedges
malt vinegar, to serve

To make the beer batter, stir together the flour, baking powder and a pinch of salt in a bowl. Gradually whisk in the beer until you have a smooth batter. Cover the bowl with cling film (plastic wrap) and chill the batter in the refrigerator until needed.

To make the tartare sauce, mix together the mayonnaise, shallot, capers, gherkins, chives and parsley. Press the hard-boiled (hard-cooked) egg through a plastic sieve (strainer) with the back of a spoon and mix into the sauce. Add a dash of Tabasco and season with salt and pepper to taste.

To make the mushy peas, put the butter in a saucepan and, when it starts to melt, add the peas. Simmer on a medium-high heat, stirring occasionally until the peas are soft. Add the mint leaves and season with salt and pepper. Reduce to a purée with a hand blender or potato masher.

To cook the fish and chips, cook the chips (fries) in a pan of boiling water for 5–6 minutes until they are not quite tender when pierced with the tip of a knife. Drain and spread out the chips in a single layer on a large plate lined with kitchen paper (paper towels). Leave for at least 20 minutes to cool.

Heat the groundnut (peanut) oil in a deep-fat fryer to 180°C/350°F and fry the chips for 4–6 minutes until they are crisp and golden brown. Drain onto a plate lined with kitchen paper and keep warm, uncovered, in a low oven.

Dip the hake fillets in the batter until coated, holding the fillets over the bowl to allow excess batter to drip back into it. Reheat the oil to 180°C/350°F and lower the fillets carefully into the hot oil. Fry for 4–6 minutes until golden brown. Lift the fish out of the oil with a skimmer and drain on a plate lined with kitchen paper.

Serve the fish and chips immediately, sprinkled lightly with salt and accompanied with the tartare sauce, mushy peas and lemon wedges to squeeze over. Serve with some malt vinegar.

FISH PIE WITH HAKE & GREEN ASPARAGUS

MAIN COURSE — SERVES 4
PREPARATION **5 MINUTES** — COOKING **1 HOUR**

In the last decade there have been great developments in freezing fish in a sustainable way. Some advantages include that the fishing is undertaken in the peak of the season and freezing is done to preserve the produce. It's affordable, transportable and easy to buy. With frozen fish you can make this fish pie any time of the year.

INGREDIENTS

600 g/1 lb 5 oz hake fillet, skinned
600 ml/1 pint/2½ cups milk
1 bay leaf
1 kg/2 lb 4 oz potatoes, peeled and cut into even-size chunks
100 g/4 oz/8 tbsp butter
freshly grated nutmeg
8 green asparagus spears (stalks), woody ends trimmed off and cut into 12.5-cm/5-in lengths, 3 stalks halved lengthwise
100 g/4 oz peas
4 tbsp plain (all-purpose) flour
handful of flat-leaf parsley, finely chopped
handful of chives, finely chopped
8 hard-boiled (hard-cooked) eggs, peeled
150 g/5 oz hard cheese, grated
salt

ALTERNATIVE FISH

haddock, pollock or cod

Preheat the oven to 180°C/350°F/Gas Mark 4. Prepare a bowl of iced water.

Place the hake fillet in a saucepan with about 500 ml/18 fl oz/2 cups of the milk, making sure the fish is submerged in the milk. Add the bay leaf and a pinch of salt. Bring the milk to the boil, turn off the heat and cover the pan. Leave to stand for about 5–7 minutes or until the fish is cooked. Drain it from the pan with a skimmer and reserve the milk but discard the bay leaf.

Bring the potatoes to the boil in a pan of lightly salted water and cook for 15–20 minutes until tender. Drain and add half the butter. Warm the remaining 100 ml/3½ fl oz/generous ⅓ cup of the milk and add as well. Mash the potatoes and season with salt, pepper and nutmeg.

Blanch the asparagus and peas for 1–2 minutes in a pan of boiling water. Drain and transfer to a bowl of iced water.

Heat the remaining 50 g/2 oz/4 tbsp butter in a saucepan over a low heat. When the butter has melted but not browned, take the pan off the heat and stir in the flour until smooth. Put the pan back on the heat and cook the flour for 1 minute, stirring with a spatula. Gradually whisk in the milk used to poach the fish (not all the milk may be needed), whisking constantly until the milk comes to the boil and you have a thick, smooth sauce. Stir in the parsley, chives, peas, whole asparagus spears (stalks) and the fish, which will break up into large chunks. Season with nutmeg, salt and pepper.

Spoon the fish mixture into a greased ovenproof dish, spreading it out in an even layer. Halve the hard-boiled (hard-cooked) eggs and press the halves into the fish mixture, spacing them out evenly. Cover with a thick layer of mashed potatoes, sprinkle with the grated cheese and arrange the halved asparagus spears on top.

Bake the pie in the oven for 20–25 minutes until the top is golden-brown.

FRIED SARDINES IN MASALA

STARTER, LUNCH — SERVES 4
PREPARATION 25 MINUTES — COOKING 5 MINUTES

Masala is the Indian word for a mix of spices and there are many variations from one region to the next. Generally, most masalas in northern India are made of dried, ground spices, while in the south, they are often liquid pastes made of fresh spices ground with water, lime juice or coconut milk. The most well-known is garam masala. Garam means hot but in the warm, rather than fiery, sense with cinnamon, cloves and black cardamom typically being used. Garam masala mixes can differ in composition and flavour from one village to another and plenty are sold today that contain 'cooling' spices such as cumin and coriander. The masala mix in this recipe is one we came across in Kollam (page 106). It's a combination of dried chillies (chiles), turmeric and black pepper. We've used it to coat a fish caught off the English coast. It's delicious!

INGREDIENTS

20 medium-size sardines,
   cleaned (see page 396)
1 tbsp ground turmeric
2 tbsp chilli powder
1 tbsp ground black pepper
1 tsp salt
coconut oil for frying

TZATZIKI

300 ml/10½ fl oz/1¼ cup
   cottage cheese or yogurt
½ cucumber, deseeded and
   finely chopped
handful of coriander (cilantro)
   leaves, finely chopped
1 garlic clove, crushed
salt and pepper

Cut the heads and tails off the sardines to prevent them burning. With a sharp knife, cut diagonal slashes 2 cm/¾ inch apart into the sardine flesh on both sides Mix together the turmeric, chilli powder, pepper and salt in a bowl. Coat the sardines all over in the spice mix and lay them on a plate.

To make the tzatziki, add all of the ingredients to a bowl and mix well. Put in the fridge for 15 minutes to allow the flavours to come together.

Heat coconut oil in a frying pan (skillet) over a medium-high heat and fry the sardines in batches on both sides for 2–3 minutes, depending on how thick they are, until golden brown.

Serve the sardines with a little of the aromatic oil from the pan drizzled over and the tzatziki on the side.

FRIED SARDINES WITH BRAISED LEEKS

I lived in Paris for a number of years and fell in love with the poireaux vinaigrette, a classic French dressing made with mustard, vinegar and oil that works very well with fried sardines. I have added a pinch of spice here which brings together the oily fish with the creamy, softened leeks.

INGREDIENTS

12 sardines, cleaned (see page 396)
1 garlic clove, finely chopped
4 leeks, trimmed and sliced into 10-cm/4-inch lengths
1 tsp Dijon mustard
1 tbsp white wine vinegar
2 sprigs of flat-leaf parsley, finely chopped
1 tsp ground piment d'Espelette
25 g/1 oz/2 tbsp butter
extra virgin olive oil
salt and pepper

With a sharp knife, cut diagonal slashes 2 cm/³⁄₄ inch apart in the flesh of the sardines on both sides. Put 3 tablespoons of olive oil and the garlic in a shallow dish, add the sardines and turn them over until they are coated in the oil. Set aside.

Put the leeks in a frying pan (skillet), just cover with lightly salted water and add the butter. Put a lid on the pan and steam the leeks over a medium heat for 10–12 minutes, stirring occasionally to prevent them sticking to the pan. Lift the leeks out of the water with tongs and cut them in half lengthwise.

Meanwhile, whisk the mustard, vinegar, parsley and 3 tablespoons of olive oil together in a bowl with a fork. Season to taste with salt and pepper.

Place a large frying pan over a high heat and fry the oil-coated sardines for 2–3 minutes on each side until golden brown. Remove from the pan.

Dress the leeks with the mustard mixture, divide between four serving plates and lay the sardines on top. Dust with a little piment d'Espelette and drizzle over a little more olive oil. Season to taste with salt.

SARDINES BAKED IN THE OVEN WITH OREGANO

MAIN COURSE — SERVES 4
PREPARATION **5 MINUTES** — COOKING 10 **MINUTES**

I love sardines for their flavour but the great thing about sardines is that you can find them all around the world, they are affordable and also extremely good for your body. High in omega 3 fatty acids and is one of the oiliest fish species, they promote good brain function and heart health.

INGREDIENTS

8 large sardines or 12 smaller sardines, cleaned (see page 396)
1 lemon, sliced
1 red chilli (chile), thinly sliced
4 garlic cloves, crushed but not skinned
10 sprigs of oregano
extra virgin olive oil
salt and pepper

Preheat the oven to 200°C/400°F/Gas Mark 6.

With a sharp knife, cut diagonal slashes 2 cm/³⁄₄ inch apart in the flesh of the sardines on both sides. Season with salt and pepper. Grease a roasting pan with olive oil and lay the sardines on it side by side. Scatter over the lemon slices, red chilli (chile) slices, garlic and most of the oregano, reserving a few sprigs for garnish. Drizzle 4 tablespoons of olive oil over the sardines and bake in the oven for 10–12 minutes. To check if the sardines are cooked, press the flesh gently and it should come away from the bones easily.

Serve garnished with the reserved oregano sprigs.

BOUILLABAISSE FROM CORNWALL

MAIN COURSE – SERVES 4
PREPARATION 10 MINUTES – COOKING 30 MINUTES

Few dishes have been discussed quite as much as bouillabaisse. Is it a soup or is it a stew? Should you drink wine with it, or absolutely not? Some people say that it can't be a bouillabaisse if it doesn't contain orange zest, while saffron is a sine qua non. In theory, any kind of fish or seafood can be added, but scorpion fish is essential as it is cooked in the soup, but served separately. Bouillabaisse is a dish from southern France, most famously associated with the port of Marseille – something everyone does seem to agree on. It originated in the fishing communities, being cooked on the beach in copper kettles over a log fire at the end of the day. It was a convenient one-pot dish that made use of all the by-catch the fishermen couldn't sell. Scorpion fish was one such fish since, rarely eaten, it was worth very little. The first time a recipe for bouillabaisse appeared in print was in a French cookbook, Le Cuisinier Durand. It called for sea bass as an ingredient, a relatively expensive fish that – like saffron – could surely not have been part of the traditional dish. In today's chic restaurant variations you can even find lobster, but one ingredient still harks back to the dish's humble origins – scorpion fish – although these days it's specially caught for bouillabaisse. In other words, it's a great fish soup recipe and that's more important than what type of fish you use or where you make it. It's just as good with hake caught off the English coast.

INGREDIENTS

ROUILLE

4 garlic cloves
1/2 tsp cayenne pepper
5 saffron threads
2 egg yolks
150 ml/5 fl oz/2/3 cup olive oil
1 tbsp lemon juice

BOUILLABAISSE

10 saffron threads
2 tbsp white wine
1 celery stick, finely chopped
1 onion, finely chopped
1/2 fennel bulb, finely sliced
2 garlic cloves, finely chopped
1 tbsp tomato purée (paste)
2 tomatoes, roughly chopped
bouquet garni (sprigs of flat-leaf
    parsley and thyme with 1 bay
    leaf, tied together with thin
    string)
2 tbsp Pernod
zest of 1/2 orange, shaved off in
    strips with a vegetable peeler
    and any pith removed
1 litre/1 3/4 pints/4 1/4 cups fish
    stock (see page 390),
400 g/14 oz potatoes, peeled
    and cut into small chunks
about 1.6 kg/3 1/2 lb total weight
    of a mixture of fish and sea-
    food, for example:
500 g/1 lb 2 oz hake, cut into
    chunks
250 g/9 oz weever fish, cleaned
500 g/1 lb 2 oz red mullet,
    cleaned
300 g/10 oz mussels, in their
    shells
salt and pepper
olive oil
1 white baguette, thinly sliced

Preheat the oven to 180°C/350°F/Gas Mark 4.

To make the rouille, crush the garlic, using a pestle and mortar, with the cayenne pepper and saffron. Transfer the mixture to a bowl and mix in the egg yolks. Whisk in the olive oil drop by drop and then add the lemon juice. Season to taste with a little salt and extra cayenne pepper. Chill the rouille in the refrigerator.

To make the bouillabaisse, crumble the saffron into the wine in a small bowl. Heat a large pan over a medium-high heat, add 2 tablespoons of olive oil and cook the celery, onion and fennel for about 4 minutes, until translucent but not browned. Add the garlic and tomato purée (paste) and fry for 2 minutes, before adding the tomatoes and bouquet garni. Stir well and leave to simmer for 2 minutes. Add the Pernod, the white wine and saffron, and add the orange zest. Bubble over a low heat until reduced by one-third and then pour in the fish stock. Add the potatoes, reduce the liquid again by one-third and turn down the heat to low.

Meanwhile, bake the baguette slices in the oven for 3–4 minutes on each side until golden brown and crisp.

Add the fish to the bouillabase, put a lid on the pan and leave to simmer over a low heat for 5–7 minutes. Uncover the pan, add the mussels, cover again and cook until all the shells have opened and the potatoes are tender. Discard any broken mussel shells or any that remain tightly closed.

Serve the soup with the rouille and baguette.

FRIED MACKEREL FILLET WITH PANZANELLA

STARTER, LUNCH — SERVES 4
PREPARATION 1 HOUR 20 MINUTES — COOKING 5 MINUTES

For years, in the fishing port of Peterhead in northern Scotland, boats have been docking every day packed with fat, super-fresh mackerel. With their sustainable fishing methods and a healthy stock of fish, its fisheries have received an MSC certificate.

INGREDIENTS

1 stale ciabatta (1 or 2 days old), cut into rough chunks
5 tbsp white wine vinegar
4 tomatoes, roughly chopped
1 red onion, finely chopped
handful of basil leaves, roughly chopped
4 x 100-g/4-oz fresh mackerel fillets or 8 smaller mackerel fillets, skin on
extra virgin olive oil
groundnut (peanut) oil, for frying
salt and pepper

ALTERNATIVE FISH
sardines, salmon steak

Put the chunks of ciabatta in a bowl and spoon over the white wine vinegar. Leave to marinate for at least 15 minutes. Add the tomatoes, red onion and basil and drizzle over some olive oil. Season with salt and pepper and mix well. Cover the bowl with cling film (plastic wrap) and set aside for 1 hour to give the flavours time to develop.

Season the mackerel fillets with salt and pepper. Heat 2 tablespoons of groundnut (peanut) oil in a frying pan (skillet)over a high heat and lay the mackerel fillets in the pan in a single layer, skin-side down. After 1 minute, turn down the heat to medium-high and if the fillets start to curl up, push them down with a spatula without moving them around. Turn the fillets over after 2 minutes, fry for another 1 minute and then remove them from the pan.

Serve the panzanella with the mackerel fillets on top, drizzled with a little olive oil.

MACKEREL ESCABECHE

STARTER, LUNCH — SERVES 4
COOKING 15 MINUTES

Although escabeche is thought of as a Spanish dish, it's actually common all round the Mediterranean. In France it is called escabèche, in Italy it's scapece and in Algeria scabetch. While the dish comes in many forms, it usually consists of fried fish with a sharp-flavoured marinade poured over it, something that may originally have been done to preserve the fish. The fish is first left to cool and then steeped in a mixture of vinegar and herbs. Sometimes the marinade is hot, sometimes sweet and sour, sometimes thickened with some dry breadcrumbs, but it always contains vinegar. Here we're cooking the fish directly in the marinade and letting everything cool together. It's easy to do and the result is delicious.

INGREDIENTS

1 garlic clove, finely chopped
1 onion, thinly sliced
1 fennel bulb, thinly sliced
2 small carrots, thinly sliced
3 bay leaves
1 tsp sugar
2 tsp coriander seeds
1 tsp fennel seeds
300 ml/10 fl oz/1¼ cups dry white wine
150 ml/5 fl oz/⅔ cup orange juice
zest of 1 orange, removed in strips using a vegetable peeler
3 tbsp white wine vinegar
8 x 65–90-g/2½–3½-oz fresh mackerel fillets, skin on
olive oil
salt and pepper

ALTERNATIVE FISH
mullet

Preheat the oven to 170°C/325°F/Gas Mark 3.

Put 2 tablespoons of olive oil in a pan over a medium-high heat, add the garlic, onion, fennel and carrots and as soon as the vegetables start to sizzle, add the bay leaves, sugar, coriander seeds and fennel seeds. Season with salt and pepper to taste. Stir-fry for 2 minutes. Add the white wine, orange juice, orange zest and vinegar and bring to the boil. Reduce the heat and simmer for 5 minutes to allow the flavours to combine. Lift out the orange zest and discard.

Lay the mackerel fillets skin-side up in an oven dish and pour over the hot marinade. Cook in the oven for 4–6 minutes.

Although the escabeche should be served lukewarm, it also tastes good served chilled.

CELERIAC SOUP WITH SMOKED MACKEREL

STARTER, LUNCH — SERVES 4
COOKING 30 MINUTES

Mackerel is another oily fish that is perfect for smoking. For this recipe you could either used cold-smoked or hot-smoked mackerel. Both work excellently with the creamy celeriac. Cold smoking requires more salt than hot smoking where the fish is lightly cooked by the heat. Take care adding salt as a seasoning as the level will vary based on the smoking process.

INGREDIENTS

1 onion, finely chopped
1 leek, white part only, finely sliced
1 celery stick, finely chopped
1 head of celeriac, peeled and diced
1 litre/1 ¾ pints/4¼ cups vegetable or chicken stock
125 ml/4 fl oz/½ cup double (heavy) cream
200 g/7 oz smoked mackerel fillet, skinned and broken into pieces
handful of chervil, finely chopped
light olive oil, for frying
extra virgin olive oil, for drizzling
salt and pepper

ALTERNATIVE FISH

hot smoked salmon

Heat 2 tablespoons of light olive oil in a large saucepan over a medium-high heat. Add the onion, leek, celery and celeriac and fry for a few minutes without letting the vegetables brown. Pour in the stock, bring to the boil and simmer for 20 minutes.

Purée the soup in a liquidizer or with a hand blender. Return it to pan, stir in the cream and reduce the soup slowly over a low heat for 5 minutes. Season with salt and pepper.

Ladle the soup into four serving bowls and divide the smoked mackerel pieces between them. Garnish the soup with chervil and a drizzle of extra virgin olive oil with some pepper ground over.

BRUFUT

BANJUL

GAMBIA

SOLE

BRUFUT, GAMBIA — 13°23'4.1"N 16°45'10.6"W
FAO 34 ATLANTIC OCEAN E
FISHERMEN — MODOU & DAWDA

A BEACH FULL
OF FISH AND
FOOTBALL SHIRTS

—⊂⊃—

As soon as the fishing boats begin to return, a colourful spectacle starts to unfold on the beach at Brufut on the Gambian coast. The small wooden boats are decorated with African motifs and almost all the crews sport the shirts of European football clubs. Occasionally you'll spot an Ajax shirt but Barcelona and Manchester United are more popular.

Men, women and children walk backwards and forwards in the breaking waves, bringing the fish ashore. The men also wear soccer shirts, while the women are in colourful dresses, carrying yellow and blue plastic baskets on their heads, many also with babies or toddlers on their backs. Some of the men use wheelbarrows or carts pulled by a donkey. Teenagers mill around as well, earning money to pay for their school fees by working as porters to carry the fish.

Onshore the fish dealers are waiting, sitting among the boat builders, net menders and lifeguards. Here and there, corn cobs are roasted over an open fire and fresh fruit and plastic bags of water are being sold. Workers slake their thirst by piercing a bag and letting the water pour into their mouth. In the distance, the turquoise domes of a mosque rise up over the scene.

Gambia's fishing boats bring in all kinds of fish – prawns (shrimp), cuttlefish, octopus, sardines and mackerel. Bycatch is not a term they use here as everything gets sold but the majority of the fish landed is Atlantic sole. There are actually two types of sole, a dark red one called a tonguefish and a more streamlined banded sole that's also known as a tiger sole or black-tip sole. There is little difference in flavour between them but both are more tender than the North Sea sole we're more familiar with, and their taste is certainly no less inferior.

Skipper Modou Mbye set out this morning at 6am with a crew of three on board. Apart from the outboard motor, there's no equipment on the boat but he knows exactly where to find the red flags marking where he cast his nets yesterday. Two fishermen at a time haul the nets aboard, taking it in turns as when the 2 km/1 ¼ mile long nets are full of fish it's gruelling work. While two haul in the nets, the other two remove the catch and fold up the nets neatly, while surprisingly big pelicans try to steal the fish. The profits are shared equally so, whatever the day's catch fetches, the money is divided into eight, with each person receiving one share. The balance goes towards the cost of maintaining the equipment – one part for the boat, one for the motor and two for the nets. In all there are around five hundred fishing boats in Gambia, spread between four landing stages. In 2012, with an eye to MSC certification, each of Gambia's landing stages was placed under the supervision of a fish manager. These managers ensure the fish is put on ice immediately to guarantee its freshness. They also keep a register that records the catches. The existing nets are gradually being replaced with newer ones that have a wider mesh and each year, between May and October, no one fishes within a mile of the coast as that's where the sole spawn. In the relatively shallow waters offshore there's plenty of food, and so lots of fish. Large industrial ships from China and Russia invade Gambia's territorial waters and pose a huge problem for the local fishing communities as, apart from emptying the sea of fish, they also often pull up the nets the African boats have cast.

Any fish not sold straight away is smoked in wooden huts. This is usually bonga, an African fish with a yellow tail. It's salted and dried in the sun, before being smoked over an open fire, sometimes for as long as twelve hours, meaning the fish can be kept indefinitely in the tropical heat. As plumes of smoke rise from the huts, the crews drag their boats onto the beach for the night. That, too, is done in the old-fashioned way with the crews making an improvised conveyor belt by rolling the boats on logs, continually moving the last one to the front. In this way the boats move up the beach one by one.

GAMBIAN DOMODA WITH FRIED SOLE

MAIN COURSE — SERVES 4
PREPARATION 5 MINUTES — COOKING 50 MINUTES

Domoda is the Gambian version of a dish that you will find throughout Africa south of the Sahara. It's a stew with a peanut sauce and is made with vegetables and usually either meat or fish, but here in Brufut, they make domoda with sole. In Holland we can easily make the same dish using peanut butter. Sole is a funny fish. Take a close look and you'll see it's a bit odd. Sole is a flatfish, like turbot and plaice, and lives on the seabed, hidden under a thin layer of sand, ready to pounce on its prey. Flatfish were ordinary-looking fish that somewhere in the distant evolutionary past learned to swim on their side (lying as flat as possible on the seabed). In the process one eye slid over to join the eye on the other side to become the top of the sole. The two eyes protrude above the sand side by side and alert to prey, while the sole's mouth and stomach did not move positions and remain on what is now the underside, giving the fish its peculiar appearance.

INGREDIENTS

1 large onion, finely chopped
3 garlic cloves, finely chopped
2 Madame Jeannette chillies (chiles) or another very hot chilli (chile) such as habanero or Scotch bonnet, halved lengthwise, deseeded and finely chopped
2 tsp tomato purée (paste)
1 x 400-g/14½-oz can plum tomatoes, coarsely chopped
100 g/4 oz/½ cup peanut butter
250 ml/8 fl oz/1 cup chicken stock
250 g/9 oz squash, peeled and deseeded weight, roughly chopped
4 x 300–400-g/10–14-oz soles, or 8 smaller soles, heads and skin removed
groundnut (peanut) oil for frying
salt

ALTERNATIVE FISH

plaice or dab

To make the domoda sauce, heat 2 tablespoons of groundnut oil in a large pan and sauté the onion until it starts to brown. Add the garlic and chillies (chiles) and fry for 30 seconds. Add the tomato purée (paste) and stir continuously over the heat for 1 minute. Add the tomatoes and cook for 3 minutes.

Add the peanut butter, stir well and then pour in the stock. Bring to the boil, cover the pan and lower the heat. Simmer for 15 minutes, stirring every few minutes.

Add the squash and simmer for about 20 minutes or until the pieces are very tender when pierced with a skewer. Season to taste with salt and leave over a low heat. If the consistency of the domoda is too thick, stir in some water or extra stock.

Pat the soles dry with kitchen paper (paper towels) and season both sides with salt and pepper. Heat 2 cm/¾ inch of groundnut (peanut) oil in a large frying pan (skillet) over a high heat and fry the fish on each side for 4–5 minutes until golden brown.

Drain the soles from the pan and serve with the domoda sauce.

SOLE À LA MEUNIÈRE

MAIN COURSE – SERVES 4
PREPARATION **5 MINUTES** – COOKING **30 MINUTES**

My grandmother lived to be a hundred. I loved her dearly and she was a wonderful cook. From the age of six I would often go out with her to eat at Van der Toren restaurant in Scheveningen. These days it attracts a lot of tourists but Grandma liked it there because she said they made her favourite dish – fried sole – better than anywhere else. Sole à la meunière is its classic French name, meaning 'cooked in the style of the miller', as the fish is first lightly coated in flour to give it a crunchy crust. Sole à la meunière is fried in butter, which adds a delicious flavour, and the butter makes a sauce. For a proper crust, you must fry the sole over a high heat but that burns the butter. The classic French recipe says to start by clarifying the butter but there is an easier way. You can begin frying the sole in oil, and add the butter to the pan at the end, thereby ensuring you still have that superb taste. As the saying goes, there's more than one way to skin a cat.

INGREDIENTS

600 g/1 lb 5 oz baby new
 potatoes, peeled
4 x 400–500-g/14-oz–1 lb 2-oz
 soles, skinned and heads
 removed or left on, as
 preferred
50 g/2 oz/scant ½ cup plain
 (all-purpose) flour, sifted
100 g/4 oz/8 tbsp butter
 (75 g/3 oz/6 tbsp for the sauce
 and 25 g/1 oz/2 tbsp for the
 potatoes)
2 handfuls of flat-leaf parsley,
 finely chopped
1 lemon
groundnut (peanut) oil for frying
salt and pepper

Put the potatoes in a pan of lightly salted water and bring to the boil. Cook for 10–15 minutes or until tender. Drain and keep warm in a low oven, covered with foil.

Coat the soles all over in the flour, brushing off any excess. Season on both sides with salt and pepper. Heat some groundnut (peanut) oil for shallow frying in a large frying pan (skillet) over a high heat and fry the soles, one at a time, for 4–6 minutes on each side until golden brown. Transfer the soles to the oven as they cook to keep them warm. Test to see if they are cooked by pressing the backbone with a spoon and the flesh should come away easily.

When all the soles have been fried, pour off the oil from the pan but don't clean it.

Add 75 g/3 oz/6 tbsp of the butter to the pan and turn off the heat. The heat the pan retains is sufficient to finish making the sauce. As soon as the butter melts and bubbles, squeeze in the juice from the lemon and add half the chopped parsley. Stir well and leave the sauce in the pan for 30 seconds.

Toss the potatoes with the remaining 25 g/1 oz/2 tbsp of butter and the rest of the parsley. Season to taste with salt.

Serve the soles with the sauce spooned over and accompanied by the potatoes.

ASIAN SOLE TIRADITO

CANAPÉ, STARTER, LUNCH — SERVES 4
PREPARATION 15 MINUTES

There are many Japanese people living in Peru. We know the Peruvian ceviche well, where fish is marinated before serving, but tiradito sees the fish prepared in a sashimi style where it is served with the marinade poured over.

INGREDIENTS

MARINADE
juice of 4 limes
300 ml/10 fl oz/1 1/4 cups yuzu
  juice
3 tbsp soy sauce
2 tbsp fish sauce

SAUCE
1 tbsp mayonnaise
1 tbsp amarillo paste (you can
  use a more intense chilli paste
  if you prefer but reduce the
  amount by half)

OTHER INGREDIENTS
350 g/12 oz sole fillets
2 tbsp sesame oil
2 tbsp extra virgin olive oil
3 sprigs of basil, leaves pulled
  from the stalks
2 spring onions (scallions),
  trimmed and finely sliced
1 chilli (chile), deseeded and
  thinly sliced
1/2 tbsp finely chopped fresh
  chives

ALTERNATIVE FISH
plaice, tuna or salmon

To make the marinade, reserve a little of the lime juice and whisk the rest of the ingredients together and set aside.

To make the sauce, stir together the mayonnaise, amarillo paste and the reserved lime juice.

Cut the fish diagonally into very thin slices, about 3–4 mm/ 1/8–1/4 inch thick, holding the fish steady with your other hand as you cut.

Arrange the slices of fish side by side on a platter or serving dish and pour over the marinade. Leave for 3–4 minutes for the flavours to develop, before drizzling over the sesame oil and olive oil. Top the fish with the amarillo mayonnaise and serve garnished with the basil leaves, sliced spring onions (scallions), chilli (chile) slices and chives.

FISH TORTILLAS

CANAPÉ, LUNCH, MAIN COURSE — SERVES 4
PREPARATION **45 MINUTES** — COOKING **5 MINUTES**

We made these fish tortillas with sole in the Gambia but you can use any fish you'd like. Just make sure the oil in the deep fryer is hot enough to make it crispy!

INGREDIENTS

BATTER

150 g/5 oz/1 cup plain
  (all-purpose) flour, sifted
1 tsp baking powder
200 ml/7 fl oz/scant 1 cup milk
1 egg, beaten

SAUCE

3 tbsp natural yogurt
3 tbsp crème fraîche (sour cream)
finely grated zest and juice of
  1 lemon
1 tsp horseradish cream
4 mint leaves, finely chopped

SALSA

2 tomatoes, deseeded and cut
  into small dice
2 garlic cloves, finely chopped
1 spring onion (scallion),
  trimmed and finely sliced
handful of coriander (cilantro)
  leaves, finely chopped
extra virgin olive oil

OTHER INGREDIENTS

8 small tortilla wraps
600 g/1 lb 5 oz sole fillets, cut
  into 5-cm/2-inch pieces
8 lettuce leaves
1 red onion, thinly sliced
1 avocado, peeled, pitted and
  diced
2 jalapeño chillies (chiles),
  thinly sliced
finely grated zest of 1 lime
lime wedges
4 sprigs of coriander (cilantro),
  leaves pulled off their stalks
  and roughly chopped
groundnut (peanut) oil for
  deep-frying
salt and pepper

ALTERNATIVE FISH

plaice or dab

To make the batter, stir the flour and baking powder together in a large bowl. Whisk in the milk gradually to avoid lumps forming and then add the egg, beating until you have a smooth batter. Season with a pinch of salt, cover the bowl with cling film (plastic wrap) and chill the batter in the refrigerator for 30 minutes.

To make the sauce, mix together the yogurt, crème fraîche (sour cream), lemon zest, lemon juice, horseradish and mint until evenly combined, season with salt and pepper and set aside.

To make the salsa, mix together the diced tomatoes, garlic, spring onion (scallion) and coriander (cilantro) with a dash of olive oil and season with salt and pepper. Set aside.

Heat some groundnut (peanut) oil in a deep-fat fryer or deep saucepan to 180°C/350°F.

Heat the wraps in a dry frying pan (skillet) for 1 minute on each side. Remove from the pan and keep warm.

Pat the pieces of fish dry with kitchen paper (paper towels) and season with salt and pepper. Dip the fish in the batter until coated and deep-fry for 3–4 minutes until golden brown and crisp. Drain from the pan onto a plate lined with kitchen paper.

Lay the tortillas on a board or plate and top each with a lettuce leaf, followed by the fried fish, spoonfuls of salsa, onion slices, avocado and jalapeño slices. Fold the tortillas in half to enclose the filling, scatter over the lime zest and serve with the sauce, chopped coriander and lime wedges to squeeze over.

THAI FISH CAKES WITH SWEET CHILLI SAUCE

CANAPÉ, STARTER — SERVES 4
PREPARATION 15 MINUTES — COOKING 10 MINUTES

I made these fishcakes on the Gambian coast using Atlantic sole. They were extremely tasty but you can easily make them with other types of fish. If you use North Sea sole, however, it could work out a rather expensive dish so choose something else. It will be just as delicious and the recipe will be the same.

INGREDIENTS

FISH CAKES (MAKES ABOUT 12)

handful of coriander (cilantro) leaves
500 g/1 lb 2 oz sole fillets, skinned and cut into chunks
1 egg
2 tbsp red curry paste (see page 291)
2 tbsp fish sauce
1 red chilli (chile), deseeded and finely chopped, plus extra chilli slices to garnish
2 spring onions (scallions), trimmed and finely chopped
75 g/3 oz green (French) beans, finely chopped
finely grated zest and juice of 1/2 lime
4 kaffir lime leaves, finely chopped
panko or dry breadcrumbs
groundnut (peanut) oil for frying

SAUCE

2 red chillies (chiles), seeds left in, roughly chopped
1 garlic clove, roughly chopped
125 g/4 oz/1/2 cup sugar
100 ml/3½ fl oz/generous 1/3 cup rice vinegar
salt

ALTERNATIVE FISH

cod, plaice or pollock

To make the fish cakes, reserve some of the coriander (cilantro) leaves for garnish and finely chop the rest. Blitz the fish, egg, red curry paste, fish sauce and chopped coriander together in a food processor. Transfer the mixture to a bowl and stir in the chopped chilli (chile), spring onions (scallions), green (French) beans, lime zest, juice and lime leaves. Mix in enough panko or dry breadcrumbs to make the mixture a bit drier and then shape it into 12 flat cakes. Place the cakes on a board or plate, cover them with cling film (plastic wrap) and chill in the refrigerator for 1 hour.

To make the sauce, grind the chillies and garlic together in a pestle and mortar. Transfer to a saucepan, add the sugar, rice vinegar, 1 tablespoon of water and salt to taste. Simmer, stirring frequently, until the sauce has a syrupy consistency. Leave to cool and then chill in the refrigerator.

Heat 2 cm/1/2 inch of groundnut (peanut) oil in a frying pan (skillet) over a high heat and fry the fish cakes on each side for 3–4 minutes until golden brown. Remove from the pan and drain on a plate lined with kitchen paper (paper towels). If you need to fry the cakes in batches, keep them warm in a low oven or covered with foil as they cook.

Serve the Thai fish cakes garnished with the reserved coriander and chilli slices. Accompany with the sweet chilli sauce.

FRIED SOLES WITH CAPERS, OLIVES & SUN-DRIED TOMATOES

MAIN COURSE – SERVES 4
PREPARATION 5 MINUTES – COOKING 15 MINUTES

The very first MSC-certified fishery I visited was the Hastings fishing fleet on the south coast of England. I fell in love with the small wooden boats launched daily from the beach and the way the fishermen responsibly catch their fish. Sole is readily available there.

INGREDIENTS

rind from ¼ lemon
1 garlic clove, thinly sliced
6 pitted black olives, thinly sliced
1 tbsp capers
1 tbsp roughly chopped sun-dried tomatoes (well drained first if in oil)
1 tbsp roughly chopped flat-leaf parsley
8 small soles, cleaned
1–2 handfuls of rocket (arugula) leaves
extra virgin olive oil
groundnut (peanut) oil, for frying
salt and pepper

Cut away the white pith from the lemon rind and discard. Slice the zest into thin julienne strips.

Heat 2 tablespoons of olive oil in a frying pan (skillet), add the garlic, olives, capers and sun-dried tomatoes and fry for 2 minutes. Add the strips of lemon zest and the parsley and season with salt and pepper.

Heat a little groundnut (peanut) oil in a large frying pan over a high heat. Season the soles all over with salt and pepper and fry the fish in batches for 3–4 minutes on each side until cooked. When the flesh comes away easily from the top of the backbone, the sole is done.

Place two soles on each serving plate, add a spoonful of the caper mixture and a few rocket (arugula) leaves. Drizzle with olive oil and serve.

EXMOUTH

CANBERRA

AUSTRALIA

PRAWNS (SHRIMP)

EXMOUTH, AUSTRALIA — 21°56'40.3"S 114°7'52.7"E

FAO 57 INDIAN OCEAN E

FISHERMEN — LENNY, FRANKLIN & ALAN

PRAWNS FROM
THE PENINSULA

—————— 🦐 ——————

Exmouth lies on a peninsula that juts out into the Pacific at the far northwesterly tip of Australia. This small town, two hours from Perth by plane, is quite isolated and for a long time was a military base belonging to the US Air Force. Since the Americans left in the early 1990s, the town has relied on tourism and fishing. The surrounding area does not have much else to offer and no one seems to have set foot on the beach there for more than twenty years.

Exmouth Gulf is the bay beside the peninsula, full of the biggest and most beautiful prawns (shrimp). It is unspoilt, surrounded by tall grasses and palm trees, and no industry means no pollution, so the water of the gulf is fantastically clean. Each season, rains wash fresh nutrients from the mud flats into the bay and the sea grass along the coast provides shelter, the perfect conditions for prawns to mature and develop in flavour.

All prawns fished at Exmouth Gulf are MSC-certified. The gulf is divided into zones, with a substantial part of it, mainly along the coast, designated the nursery area where fishing is not allowed. It gives the young prawns the peaceful environment they need to mature undisturbed among the mangroves and sea grass. In theory, unlimited fishing is allowed in the other zones during the season, which runs from April to December, but those zones may be closed if the prawn stocks are in danger of being depleted.

These restrictions are pretty easy to enforce as there are only six boats operating in the gulf and they all belong to the same company, MG Kailis. Senior skipper Len Franklin has been fishing here for prawns for 41 years. In that time, he says, the fishing methods have barely changed. When he started, they still used sailing boats, before moving on to converted lobster fishing vessels, but never without a trawl. Nowadays, several nets up to 2 metres/6½ feet deep hang from the steel arms that extend from either side of the boat. They are so big the fishermen can walk across them.

Captain Len fishes for three varieties of prawn – tiger prawns (shrimp), king prawns (jumbo shrimp) and Endeavour prawns (shrimp). Each is quite distinct in appearance. The Endeavour is yellow, the king is more transparent and the tiger prawn is banded with dark stripes across its back, hence its name. They all have a different flavour and are good to eat. Len explains that tiger prawns are in a class of their own, great for impressing the in-laws! If you're entertaining friends, serve the king prawns, while Endeavours are perfect for making yourself a sandwich. They are slightly smaller, which means you have to peel a few more, but that just makes eating them all the more rewarding.

The prawn fishing season means working a seven-day, or rather seven-night, week. Prawns are nocturnal creatures, so fishing is carried out at night when they are active. The prawns grow a little bigger with each new lunar cycle, when they move further out to sea. Each type of prawn has its own migration route but you can never be sure where to find them. It always comes down to a combination of guesswork and searching, but this is where Len Franklin benefits from his 41 years' experience.

During the prawn season, the fishermen stay on the vessel day and night. Previously when there was a full moon and the prawns were inactive because of the light, the fishermen would have just this one night off once a month. Len laughs when he tells us that traditionally it was the night when the men went into town to fill their bellies, fight and chase women. He claims it's where the phrase 'full moon party' comes from. Nowadays, the men don't just have the one night off when there's a full moon, but five days, as this takes the pressure off the prawn stocks.

The Exmouth fishermen say that you don't need to do anything to a good prawn. A truly wild prawn is so full of flavour that all it needs is a wedge of lemon and a pinch of white pepper, which is exactly how they eat them in Exmouth.

For the past five years the prawns have been frozen on board, ensuring that when they reach the factory, they don't get mixed up with prawns caught by other vessels or in other waters. You can ask for Len's prawns specifically at a market in Perth, which is important as not all types of prawn taste the same. Their flavour is determined by the waters in which they swim, how active they are and their food source. In fact, it's just like wine, with every prawn having its own *terroir*, in which case Len Franklin's from the Exmouth Gulf are the equivalent of a shellfish *Grand Cru*.

GAMBAS A LA PLANCHA

MAIN COURSE — SERVES 4
PREPARATION 10 MINUTES — COOKING 5 MINUTES

When it comes to prawns (shrimp), no dish is more famous than gambas a la plancha – king prawns (jumbo shrimp), still in their shells, fried in a layer of sea salt in a red hot pan. The salt spreads the heat evenly so the prawn shells become crisp while the meat inside steams in its own juices. Large fresh prawns are by far the tastiest when cooked this way as it's just the prawns you taste – and nothing else.

INGREDIENTS

AIOLI

2 garlic cloves
1 egg
100 ml/3½ fl oz/generous ⅓ cup sunflower oil
100 ml/3½ fl oz/generous ⅓ cup extra virgin olive oil
2 tsp lemon juice

GAMBAS

250 g/9 oz/generous ¾ cup fine sea salt
20 raw king prawns (jumbo shrimp), unpeeled with heads and tails left on
salt and pepper

To make the aioli, crush the garlic in a pestle and mortar. Whisk the egg into the crushed garlic (if the mortar is too small for the egg and oils to be added, first transfer the garlic to a bowl).

Add the sunflower and olive oils drop by drop, whisking constantly. When both oils have been emulsified into the egg and garlic, season the mixture with the lemon juice, salt and pepper. Chill the aioli in the refrigerator until ready to serve.

To cook the gambas, spread the sea salt in an even layer about 5 mm/¼ inch thick over a large frying pan (skillet) or plancha (flat, cast-iron griddle). Place the pan over the heat and when it is really hot, arrange the prawns (shrimp) over the salt, pressing them down lightly. Cook for 3–5 minutes, depending on the thickness of the prawns, turning them over once with two spatulas and pressing them down again into the salt. When cooked, remove the prawns from the pan and brush excess salt off them.

Serve the prawns with the aioli as a dip. Give each diner a small bowl of warm water with a slice of lemon added so they can rinse their fingers as they eat.

TOM YUM KUNG WITH THAI BASIL

STARTER, LUNCH — SERVES 4
COOKING 15 MINUTES

Prawns (shrimp) have a strong enough flavour to cope with the addition of fiery Asian root spices like the galangal and ginger from the red curry paste. While the meaty texture works well with the creaminess of the coconut milk. Tom Yang Kung is super-quick to make and packed with flavour.

INGREDIENTS

2 tbsp red curry paste (see page 291)
1 lemongrass stalk, crushed and chopped
1 tbsp peeled and sliced fresh galangal root
3 kaffir lime leaves
250 ml/8 fl oz/1 cup coconut milk
1 litre/1 ¾ pints/4¼ cups shell-fish stock (see page 390)
350 g/12 oz large raw prawns (shrimp), peeled and deveined (see page 395)
150 g/5 oz sugar snap peas, ends and edges trimmed
200 g/7 oz oyster mushrooms, sliced
100 g/3½ oz bean sprouts
handful of Thai basil leaves, coarsely chopped
handful of coriander (cilantro) leaves, coarsely chopped
1 small red chilli (chile), deseeded, thinly sliced
1 lime, cut into wedges
groundnut (peanut) oil for frying
salt

Heat a little groundnut (peanut) oil in a large pan over a medium-high heat, add the curry paste and fry for 1 minute.

Add the lemongrass, galangal, lime leaves, coconut milk and stock. Bring to the boil and add the prawns (shrimp) and sugar snap peas, Turn the heat down to low and leave to simmer for 3 minutes.

Lastly add the oyster mushrooms and cook for a further 3 minutes. Season with salt and pepper to taste.

Ladle the soup into four bowls and serve topped with the bean sprouts, Thai basil, coriander (cilantro) and chilli (chile) slices. Accompany with lime wedges to squeeze over.

PIRI PIRI PRAWNS WITH MANGO & PADRÓN PEPPERS

CANAPÉ, STARTER — SERVES 4
PREPARATION 5 MINUTES — COOKING 35 MINUTES

We all think the term 'Piri Piri' comes from Portugal but originally it was the Portuguese who brought it from America to Mozambique. 'Piri' meaning 'chilli' in Swahili. But in Mozambique they make piri piri dishes sweeter by adding mango to the base which gives a perfect spicy sweetness to the butterflied prawns (shrimp).

INGREDIENTS

4 garlic cloves, finely chopped
300 g/10 oz/1¼ cups rice
600 g/1 lb 5 oz raw king prawns
    (jumbo shrimp), peeled, heads
    and tails left on and deveined
    (see page 395)
1 tbsp paprika
1 onion, roughly chopped
2 chillies (chiles), finely sliced
1 mango, peeled and flesh diced
2 limes
2 tbsp extra virgin olive oil
6 sprigs of coriander (cilantro),
    leaves pulled from stalks
20 g/¾ oz/1½ tbsp butter
300 g/10 oz padrón peppers
groundnut (peanut) oil, for
    frying
light olive oil, for frying
salt and pepper

Heat a little groundnut (peanut) oil in a saucepan and sauté 1 clove of finely chopped garlic for 2–3 minutes without letting it brown. Add the rice and stir for 30 seconds and then pour in enough cold water to come 1 cm/½ inch above the rice. Bring to the boil, cover the pan and simmer for 10 minutes, by which time the rice should have absorbed all the water. Take the pan off the heat and, with the lid left on, leave the rice to stand for 10 minutes.

Butterfly the prawns (shrimp) by cutting them open lengthwise but without cutting them completely in half. Sprinkle the prawns with the paprika and set aside.

Heat a little groundnut oil in another pan and fry the remaining 3 cloves of garlic, onion and chilli (chile) for a few minutes until softened. Add the mango and the juice of half a lime. Stir well and fry for another 2–3 minutes. Tip the contents of the pan into the bowl of a blender or food processor, add the olive oil and liquidize or process until smooth. Season with salt.

Heat 2 tablespoons of light olive oil and the butter in a frying pan (skillet) over a high heat. Fry the prawns until they are browned on all sides, turning them over every 30 seconds and taking care not to overcook them. Remove the prawns from the pan.

Heat 2 tablespoons of light olive oil in a second frying pan and fry the padrón peppers for about 5 minutes, stirring and turning them over occasionally. Season with a pinch of salt.

Serve the fried prawns with the sauce, garnished with the coriander (cilantro) leaves. Accompany with the padrón peppers, rice and any leftover limes served separately.

PRAWNS FROM THE BARBIE WITH BLACK PEPPER SAUCE

LUNCH, MAIN COURSE — SERVES 4
PREPARATION 10 MINUTES — COOKING 20 MINUTES

I love open-fire, outdoor cooking and seafood is wonderful served straight from the 'barbie'. Australians love it. I made this dish for the fishermen when we came back from our nightly trip hunting for prawns (shrimp).

INGREDIENTS

12 whole large tiger prawns (jumbo shrimp)
1 tbsp whole black peppercorns
1/2 tbsp whole white peppercorns
1/2 tbsp whole red peppercorns
1 red chilli (chile), deseeded and sliced into rings
2 garlic cloves, finely chopped
3 1/2 tablespoons unsalted butter
1 tbsp oyster sauce
1 tbsp fish sauce
1-cm/1/8-inch piece of root ginger, peeled
1/2 tsp sugar
100 ml/1/3 cup chicken stock
2 handfuls of rocket (arugula)
5 chives, finely cut
2 spring onions (scallions), sliced into rings
handful of coriander (cilantro) leaves
vegetable oil
salt and pepper
lime wedges, to serve

Place the prawns (shrimp) in a large bowl and add 2 tablespoons of vegetable oil, plus a little salt and pepper. Mix well and set aside to marinate.

Grind all of the peppercorns in a mortar using a pestle to break them up.

Toast the black, white and red peppercorns in a dry frying pan (skillet) set over a high heat for about 1 minute until they start smoking. Remove from the pan and set aside.

Take the pan off the heat for a moment and add 1 tablespoon of vegetable oil. Return the toasted peppercorns to the pan with the garlic and chilli and fry for 1–2 minutes. Next, add the butter. As soon as the butter is melted, add the oyster sauce, fish sauce and mix in the ginger. Now add the sugar, mix well, and then add the chicken stock. Reduce the sauce until it becomes thick. Give the sauce a taste, season with salt if you wish, set apart and keep warm.

Preheat the barbecue (grill) to a medium-high heat. Grill the marinated prawns for 2–3 minutes on each side and make sure they do not overcook.

Arrange half of the rocket (arugula) on a platter and place the prawns on top. Drizzle the sauce over the top.

Dress four serving plates with the chives, spring onions (scallions), coriander leaves, the rest of the rocket ready to add the prawns. Serve with lime wedges to squeeze over.

SPRING ROLLS

CANAPÉ, STARTER, LUNCH — SERVES 4
PREPARATION **20 MINUTES** — COOKING **15 MINUTES**

While in Europe we use salted anchovies as a flavour enhancer, in Asia they use fish sauce. Some fish sauces can take up to two years to ferment – as they do so, amino acids develop to produce that deep, savoury umami flavour (see page 315). Although Asian cuisines have made us familiar with this type of sauce today, they were, in fact, enjoyed in Europe in ancient times. The Greeks made garos, while the Romans made garum or liquamen, fermenting salted fish (innards and all) for months in the sun until they disintegrated, before straining the residue. Garum is used in almost all recipes recorded by the Roman gourmet Apicius, after whom one of the earliest cookbooks was named. These sauces were used in Europe until well into the sixteenth century, after which garum made way for salted anchovies.

INGREDIENTS

DIP

4 tbsp fish sauce
2 tbsp rice vinegar
1 tbsp sugar
juice of 1 lime
2 garlic cloves, finely chopped
1 red chilli (chile), deseeded and
  finely chopped

SPRING ROLLS

12 asparagus spears (stalks)
1 cucumber
1 carrot
150 g/5 oz cooked prawns
  (shrimp), peeled (see page
  395)
4 spring onions (scallions),
  trimmed and cut lengthwise
  into thin strips
50 g/2 oz baby spinach leaves
50 g/2 oz bean sprouts
handful of mint leaves, chopped
handful of coriander (cilantro)
  leaves, chopped
handful of Thai basil leaves,
  chopped
150 g/5 oz glass noodles
12 rice paper wrappers
1 lime, cut into wedges

To make the dip, put the fish sauce, 4 tablespoons of water, the rice vinegar and the sugar in a saucepan and heat gently until the sugar has dissolved. Leave to cool and then stir in the lime juice, garlic and chilli (chile).

To prepare the spring rolls, blanch the asparagus spears (stalks) in a pan of lightly salted boiling water for 1 minute. Drain and rinse lightly under cold running water.

Cut the cucumber in half lengthwise, deseed and cut into matchsticks. Cut the carrot into sticks the same size as the cucumber. Lay the cucumber, carrot, prawns (shrimp), spring onions (scallions), asparagus spears, baby spinach leaves, bean sprouts and herbs in separate piles side by side on a large board.

Cook the noodles in a large pan of lightly salted boiling water according to the packet instructions. Drain in a colander and rinse lightly under cold running water so the noodles do not stick together. Transfer the noodles to a bowl and mix them with 2 tablespoons of the dip to add flavour.

To assemble the spring rolls. Dip a rice paper wrapper in a large bowl of warm water for a few seconds to soften it. Lay the wrapper on a board and top with a couple of prawns, vegetable sticks, a few spinach leaves, bean sprouts, herbs and noodles, piling everything in the middle of the wrapper. Fold in the sides of the wrapper over the filling and roll up to enclose the filling. If wished, you can just fold over one side of the wrapper so one end of the roll remains open when you roll it and you can see the filling. Repeat until you have used all the rice paper wrappers and the filling ingredients.

Serve the spring rolls with the dip and lime wedges to squeeze over.

PAD THAI

MAIN COURSE — SERVES 4
PREPARATION 15 MINUTES — COOKING 15 MINUTES

No book that claimed to be an authority of fish cooking would be complete without a recipe for pad Thai with prawns (shrimp). Wherever you are in the world you will find a prawn that could be used – they are all delicious!

INGREDIENTS

SAUCE

3 tbsp tamarind paste
2 tbsp brown sugar
6 tbsp fish sauce

NOODLES

250 g/9 oz flat rice noodles
400 g/14 oz medium-sized raw prawns (shrimp), deveined (see page 395)
4 eggs, lightly beaten
2 garlic cloves, finely chopped
1 small shallot, finely chopped
1/2 red chilli (chile), deseeded and finely chopped
1/2 head of pak choi (bok choy), roughly chopped
100 g/4 oz bean sprouts
2 spring onions (scallions), trimmed and finely sliced
4 tbsp finely chopped unsalted peanuts
1 lime, cut into wedges
handful of coriander (cilantro) leaves, finely chopped
groundnut (peanut) oil, for frying

ALTERNATIVE SHELLFISH

crayfish

To make the sauce, mix the tamarind paste, brown sugar and fish sauce together with 4 tablespoons of water in a bowl, stirring until the sugar has dissolved.

Bring a large pan of water to the boil, remove it from the heat, add the rice noodles and leave to soak for about 3 minutes until softened, or follow the instructions on the packet. Stir the noodles occasionally with a pair of tongs to keep them separate. Drain the noodles and rinse lightly under cold running water to prevent them sticking together.

Heat 2 tablespoons of groundnut (peanut) oil in a wok over a high heat, add the prawns (shrimp) and stir-fry for 1–2 minutes until they have turned a deep pink. Remove the prawns from the wok and set aside.

Add another spoonful of oil to the wok, pour in the beaten eggs and stir until the eggs are set. Remove from the wok and chop the cooked egg into small pieces.

Return the wok to a high heat, add 2 tablespoons of oil and stir-fry the garlic, shallot and chilli (chile) for 30 seconds. Tip in the noodles, pour over the sauce and stir-fry for 1–2 minutes until the noodles have absorbed the sauce. Taste to check the noodles are tender and, if the sauce is too thick, add 1 tablespoon of water. Add the prawns and chopped egg, mix well and then add the pak choi (bok choy), bean sprouts and peanuts. Stir-fry for 30 seconds.

Divide the pad thai between four serving plates and garnish with the coriander (cilantro) and lime segments to squeeze over.

AUSTRALIA – PRAWNS (SHRIMP)

NASI GORENG

MAIN COURSE — SERVES 4

PREPARATION 1 HOUR 5 MINUTES — COOKING 35 MINUTES

Meaning literally 'fried rice', nasi goreng is a national dish of Indonesia. I have travelled all around Indonesia and I love the way they cook their fish. I like the combination of lovely grilled fish with homemade sambal. This dish is traditionally served with fried eggs, prawn crackers, pickled cucumber and sambal olek to spice it up as you desire.

INGREDIENTS

ATJAR (PICKLED CUCUMBER)

150 ml/5 fl oz/²/₃ cup white
    wine vinegar
2 tbsp sugar
½ cucumber, halved lengthwise,
    deseeded and sliced

NASI GORENG

300 g/10 oz/1 ¹/₃ cups long-grain
    rice
6 eggs
1 shallot, chopped
2 garlic cloves, finely chopped
1 leek, white part only, finely
    sliced (reserve some for
    garnish)
1 red chilli (chile), deseeded and
    finely sliced
1 small head of Chinese
    cabbage, washed and finely
    shredded
1 carrot, finely diced
2 spring onions (scallions),
    trimmed and finely sliced
400 g/14 oz medium-sized raw
    prawns (shrimp), peeled and
    deveined (see page 395)
2 tbsp fish sauce
2 tbsp sweet soy sauce
2 tbsp soy sauce
4 sprigs of coriander (cilantro),
    leaves roughly chopped
prawn crackers (shrimp chips)
sambal oelek
groundnut (peanut) oil for frying
salt and pepper

ALTERNATIVE FISH

crayfish

To make the atjar, heat the vinegar and sugar in a small saucepan over a low heat, stirring until the sugar dissolves. Leave to cool and then add the cucumber slices. Leave to marinate in the refrigerator for at least 1 hour.

Cook the rice in plenty of lightly salted water, following the instructions on the packet. Leave the cooked, drained rice to steam dry in the pan. Leave to cool.

Heat a little groundnut (peanut) oil in a frying pan (skillet) over a medium-high heat and fry four of the eggs (one egg per serving). Season the eggs to taste with salt and pepper, remove them from the pan and keep warm under a sheet of foil.

Heat 2 tablespoons of groundnut oil in a wok (or large frying pan) over a high heat and stir-fry the shallot, garlic, sliced leek and chilli (chile). Add the cabbage, carrot and spring onions (scallions) and stir-fry for a further 1 minute. Push the vegetables to one side of the pan and crack in the two remaining eggs. Fry, stirring constantly, until the eggs have set. Stir the cooked egg into the vegetables, add the rice and stir-fry for 1 minute. Add the prawns (shrimp), stir-fry for 2 minutes and then pour in the fish sauce, sweet soy sauce and soy sauce and toss everything together. Stir-fry for 1 minute, taste and season with salt.

Serve the nasi goreng with the coriander (cilantro) and reserved sliced leek scattered over, topped with the fried eggs. Serve the atjar, sambal oelek and prawn crackers (shrimp chips) separately.

CHINESE PRAWN TOASTS

CANAPÉ, STARTER — SERVES 4
PREPARATION 10 MINUTES — COOKING 10 MINUTES

This is a great thing to serve as finger food at a party. You can prepare it in advance and deep-fry it quickly on demand. People love it because it has the crispiness of the toast, the nuttiness of the sesame seeds and the sweet joy of the prawn (shrimp).

INGREDIENTS

10 slices of white sandwich (pullman or pan) bread, one day old
12 large raw prawns (shrimp), peeled and deveined (see page 395)
3 tbsp soy sauce
1 tbsp sesame oil
2-cm/¾-inch piece of fresh root ginger, peeled and roughly chopped
1 egg white
3 tbsp black sesame seeds
3 tbsp white sesame seeds
groundnut (peanut) oil for deep-frying
pepper

Remove the crusts from the bread and cut the slices in half diagonally.

Put the prawns (shrimp), soy sauce, sesame oil, ginger and egg white in a food processor and process until smooth. Season lightly with pepper. Using a spoon, divide the prawn mixture between the half slices of bread, spreading the mixture in an even layer. Mix together the black and white sesame seeds and sprinkle them over the prawn mixture, pressing the seeds down lightly.

Heat some groundnut (peanut) oil for deep-frying in a deep-fat fryer or deep saucepan to 180°C/350°F, checking the oil is hot enough, either by using a cooking thermometer or by dropping a piece of bread into the oil, which should rise to the surface immediately and begin to brown.

Fry the triangles of bread in batches for 2 minutes each, prawn-side up, and then flip over and fry the other side for 1 minute, until the toasts are crisp and golden brown. Drain from the pan onto a plate lined with kitchen paper (paper towels) and serve the toasts hot or cold.

SEAFOOD PIZZA

CANAPÉ, LUNCH, MAIN COURSE — SERVES 4
PREPARATION 3 HOURS 40 MINUTES — COOKING 20 MINUTES

Seafood and pizza is a marriage made in heaven. When I think of seafood pizza I think of anchovies, tuna or whole sardines. They all work perfectly as toppings. In this version I use cockles, prawns (shrimp) and squid but try any combination of seafood that you like best.

INGREDIENTS

250 g/9 oz/1 ¾ cups strong white bread flour or Tipo 00 flour, plus extra for dusting
125 ml/4 fl oz/½ cup lukewarm water
15 g/½ oz fresh (compressed/cake) yeast or 7-g sachet fast-action dried yeast
1 x 400-g/14½-oz can of plum tomatoes
1 shallot, chopped
250 g/9 oz cockles in their shells/clams
200 g/7 oz cherry tomatoes, quartered
50 g/2 oz small raw prawns (shrimp), peeled
150 g/5 oz squid, cleaned and cut into rings (see page 401)
1 tbsp chopped fresh oregano
handful of fresh basil leaves
olive oil, for making dough, frying and greasing
chilli oil*, for drizzling
salt and pepper

Chilli oil is easy to make. Just add fresh chillies (chiles) to a bottle of good-quality olive oil, making sure the chillies are submerged in the oil. The more chillies you add and the longer you leave them in the bottle, the hotter the oil will be.

Sift the flour onto the worktop and mix in 1 teaspoon of salt and the dried yeast (if using). Shape the flour into a mound with a well in the centre. Put the lukewarm water and 1 tablespoon of olive oil in a bowl, add the fresh yeast (if using) and stir until it dissolves. Pour into the well in the flour and mix to make a dough.

Knead the dough for about 10 minutes or until it is smooth and elastic. The longer you knead, the better the dough will be. Shape it into a ball, place in a large bowl and cover the bowl with cling film (plastic wrap). Leave the dough to rise at room temperature for 3 hours by which time it should have almost doubled in size.

Blitz the plum tomatoes using a hand blender or chop them finely. Simmer the tomatoes in a saucepan for about 5 minutes or until they have thickened slightly to make a sauce. Season to taste with salt and pepper and set aside.

Heat 1 tablespoon of olive oil in a frying pan (skillet) and sauté the shallot for 2 minutes. Season with a pinch of pepper and immediately add the cockles/clams. Cover the pan and cook the cockles, shaking the pan every 30 seconds and lifting the lid occasionally to check if their shells have opened. Once they've all opened, take the pan off the heat and remove the cockle meat from the shells. Set aside.

Preheat the oven to 220°C/425°F/Gas Mark 7.

Put the ball of dough on a floured surface and knead for a couple of minutes to knock any air out of it. Roll out the dough to a large round about 5 mm/¼ inch thick. Brush a baking sheet with oil or line with baking parchment (baking paper). Lift the dough onto the sheet and press it out to the edges so the dough covers the entire baking sheet.

Spoon the tomato sauce over the dough, spreading it evenly, and arrange the cherry tomato quarters on top. In a bowl, mix 1 tablespoon of oil with the prawns (shrimp), squid and cockles until the seafood is coated. Spoon over the pizza base, scatter over the oregano and drizzle with olive oil. Bake the pizza for 10 minutes in the oven until the crust is golden brown.

Remove the pizza from the oven and scatter over the basil leaves. Serve with chilli oil to drizzle over and give the pizza a spicy flavour.

AMSTERDAM

YERSEKE

NETHERLANDS

OYSTERS, MUSSELS & RAZOR CLAMS

YERSEKE, NETHERLANDS — 51°29'34.5"N 4°2'55.2"E

FAO 27 ATLANTIC OCEAN NE

FISHERMEN — JOOP & JAN

THE FRESHEST MUSSELS EVER

Not far from the village of Yerseke in Zeeland, a province in the south-west of the Netherlands, you'll find the distribution centres of the large Dutch mussel companies, standing side by side overlooking the water. Each company has its own eatery – there are five along the road, all close together and all serving the freshest mussels. Yerseke has a large number of restaurants for a village of no more than 7,000 inhabitants, but people even come here from Belgium to feast on its mussels and oysters.

Zeeland's islands are situated in the estuaries of the Rhine-Meuse-Scheldt delta, where the rivers flow out into the North Sea. Two methods of cultivation are used here in the waters of the Eastern Scheldt, but both involve first harvesting wild mussel seed. In the soil culture technique, the seed is spread and sown within enclosed areas in the water. In the second technique – known as suspended culture – the seed is placed in stocking-like containers that are suspended in the water from poles. Below the surface it presents an amazing sight, the bundles of mussels hanging in the clear green water like huge waving beaded curtains. As soon as they are full of large mussels, the 'stockings' are lifted out of the water by boats. The mussels are not only sold fresh but are also cooked, preserved or the shells are removed and they are placed in jars. The shells are not thrown away but are then passed on to the oyster farmers.

The province is famous not only for its mussels but also for its oysters, especially the Zeeland flat oysters, with both Zeeland specialities being MSC-certified. The oysters are cultivated in the Eastern Scheldt in 'beds', where they are set out neatly by the growers. The first job is to obtain the wild oyster larvae, called alevins. The empty mussel shells are tipped out into the river where they form a ready-made bed for the alevins. Once larvae settle on the empty mussel shells, they attach themselves and grow shells of their own. The young oysters are then carefully removed by the growers and moved to the oyster beds.

The clean, clear water of the Eastern Scheldt is crucial for the flavour of the oysters. As a general rule, the saltier the water, the better the taste, but other factors affect the flavour too, such as the mineral content of the water and the abundance of plankton upon which the oysters feed. The water of the Eastern Scheldt ensures the oysters have a truly unique flavour.

When the oysters are the right size, they are moved yet again. This time they are taken into Yerseke, where, sandwiched between the houses of the historic centre, you will find shallow, square, concrete tanks covered with seawater. The famous Zeeland oysters are still kept in these oyster wells today. The oysters are sprayed with fresh seawater throughout the day fed through a simple system of pipes. Now and then a seagull manages to steal one, dropping the shell from a great height to break it, before picking out and eating the briny meat inside.

Another delicacy found along the Dutch coast and loved by seagulls – if they can get hold of them – are razor clams. This small clam gets its name from its thin, elongated shell, which looks just like an old-fashioned cut-throat razor; the shell's edges can be incredibly sharp. The clam itself is long and white and the meat inside deliciously tender and sweet, provided it is not overcooked, when it develops a rubbery texture.

The razor clam originates from the western coast of the Atlantic and was introduced along the German coast at the end of the 1970s. In no time at all the entire North Sea coastline was full of razor clams. They particularly like the clean sand of the Wadden Sea in the north of the Netherlands. Wadden Sea razor clams were MSC-certified in 2016.

Razor clams are strange little creatures that sit upright, partially buried in the sand along the shoreline. The clams inside can extend beyond the shell at both ends – at the bottom, their strong little 'feet' allow them to burrow into the wet sand in a flash, while at the top the siphon protrudes, a small pipe that allows the clams to suck in water and then filter out food and oxygen.

Commercial fisheries fish for razor clams using hydraulic dredges. They pump water into the sand, making the sand 'liquid', which allows the fishermen to dredge the bottom of the sea by up to 22 cm/8½ inches and collect the razors.

You can also catch razor clams yourself, by hand. Look carefully and you will see all kinds of small holes along the shore when the tide goes out. Just sprinkle a pinch of salt over the holes and the razors will extend their siphons because they think the tide has returned. At that point, you can pull them out of the sand with your hands but you need to be quick as, before you know it, they will have disappeared back down again.

The oysters are traditionally packed in kelp, the greenish-brown blistered tendrils of which can be found all along the dykes. Cutting kelp for the oyster trade is a time-honoured occupation in Yerseke and Jan Kruijsse continues it to this day but kelp isn't the only seaweed Jan harvests along the Eastern Scheldt. Three years ago he came across a Japanese stall at a fish trade fair where he saw all kinds of dishes made with edible seaweeds and thought, 'that stuff grows here too'. In winter, he harvests fresh wakame, recognizable by its bright green stalks in the Japanese seaweed salads sold in supermarkets, as well as Japanese wireweed and kombu. Other varieties grow in the summer, such as sea lettuce, toothed wrack and red hornweed. The edible Oriental varieties are not native to the area and were probably introduced via the

ballast water of ships from Asia, but they thrive in the clean water.

Another shellfish the Dutch are famous for is cockles, a mollusc with a salty-sweet flavour. Joop Paauwe supplies cockles from Yerseke throughout Holland and Belgium and he even delivers to restaurants in Spain. Today, most of Zeeland's cockle pickers fish in the north in the Wadden Sea but since 2005 mechanical cockle picking has been banned by the government. The cockle boats with their massive trawl nets wreaked havoc on the seabed, leaving little for the breeding birds to feed on. In the Wadden Sea it's still possible to pick cockles by hand in the old-fashioned way and the hand dredger is MSC-certified there.

Joop Paauwe is the only person licensed to pick cockles in Zeeland. He fishes in Veerse Meer, a branch of the Eastern Scheldt, using a new method involving a rectangular pallet with a conveyor belt in the centre that scrapes along the bottom. The cockles are lifted out of the sand on either side so it's mechanical fishing in miniature. Each week he fishes a different part of the water and after five weeks he's back where he started, which allows the riverbed time to recover and gives the smaller cockles that escaped through the mesh last time a chance to grow bigger.

Cockles are generally at their best in the warmer months when they have plenty to eat. In Veerse Meer there is so much food for them that Joop can pick large round cockles all year long. And there's another reason why his cockles are so good – within an hour of picking them, Joop puts them back in water to keep them in top condition. He also sorts and scoops out the nets by hand as cockles are sensitive creatures and you can't throw them around. As Joop says: 'You have to treat a shellfish as you would treat your wife!'

OYSTERS WITH BLACK BEAN SAUCE

CANAPÉ, STARTER — SERVES 4
PREPARATION 10 MINUTES — COOKING 10 MINUTES

I adore Chinese food, but my girlfriend is less keen, so when I have an evening on my own, the first thing I do is go out for a Chinese. In Amsterdam, where I live, the best area is Zeedijk, which is our Chinatown. The most famous Chinese restaurant there is Nam Kee and it's especially famous for its oysters in black bean sauce. There's even a book – and a film – called Oysters at Nam Kee's. The restaurant might not have the most romantic atmosphere – plastic tablecloths, fluorescent lighting and you order by the numbers on the menu – and it may not serve the best oysters, as they're always those big ones that you need a knife and fork to eat (everyone knows the little ones are best). But I keep going back as their oysters have the best flavour anywhere. Maybe it's just the nostalgia effect.

INGREDIENTS

24 large oysters, such as Creuse, Pacific or Japanese
3 tbsp black bean paste
finely grated zest and juice of ½ lime, plus extra juice to serve
5-cm/2-inch piece of cucumber, deseeded and cut into fine dice
¼ red chilli (chile), deseeded and finely chopped
handful of coriander (cilantro) leaves, finely chopped
coarse salt or seaweed for serving the oysters

Open the oysters using an oyster knife (see page 394). Loosen the oyster meat and reserve the liquor. Strain the liquor to remove any tiny fragments of shell. Remove the oyster meat from the shells, reserving the curved half shells and discarding the flat halves. Rinse the curved shells lightly under cold running water.

Pour the oyster liquor into a saucepan and bring to the boil. Turn off the heat and add the oysters to the pan. Leave the oysters for 2–3 minutes so they 'poach' in the warm liquor, turning them over occasionally. Drain the oysters from the pan with a slotted spoon.

Whisk the black bean paste into the warm liquor and cook for 1 minute over a low heat until the sauce has thickened. Mix in the lime juice and set aside.

Spread a layer of coarse salt or seaweed over a serving platter and press the curved shells into it to prevent them moving around. Slip an oyster into each shell and spoon over a little of the black bean sauce.

Divide the diced cucumber and red chilli (chile)between the oysters and drizzle over extra lime juice. Served garnished with chopped coriander (cilantro) and lime zest.

RAZOR CLAMS WITH SAUCE VIERGE

STARTER, LUNCH — SERVES 4
PREPARATION **10 MINUTES** — COOKING **10 MINUTES**

As long as you cook them well, razor clams taste delicious. When alive you will find them standing just under the sand and the body comes just above the sand to eat. Cook them quickly because if you cook them for too long they will become tough and you want to enjoy them while still tender and juicy, not at all tough. As long as the shells have opened they are ready to eat or to be pan-fried as here.

INGREDIENTS

16 razor clams (Atlantic Jackknife clams)
1 large ripe tomato
1 shallot, chopped
2 tbsp lemon juice
1 tbsp basil leaves in very fine strips
extra virgin olive oil for frying
salt and pepper

Give the razor clams a good rinse under cold running water.

Pour about 1 cm/½ inch of water into a large frying pan (skillet) and place over a medium-high heat. Add the clams to the pan, making sure there is enough space between the shells for them to open fully. Cover the pan and cook the clams for 3–5 minutes, depending on size, checking regularly to see if the shells have opened. As soon as all the shells are open, drain the clams from the pan and set aside to cool.

To make the sauce, cut a cross in the base of the tomato and plunge it into a pan of boiling water for 10–15 seconds. Lift out the tomato with a slotted spoon and immediately run cold water over it. Peel off the skin and leave the tomato to cool before cutting it in half, scooping out the seeds and cutting the flesh into small dice.

Heat 2 tablespoons of olive oil in a frying pan and fry the shallot for 2 minutes until translucent. Add another dash of olive oil, the diced tomato and lemon juice and season with salt and pepper. Add the basil and simmer for 1 minute over a low heat. Remove the pan from the heat and put a lid on it to keep the sauce warm.

Remove the meat from the clam shells and wash the shells thoroughly under cold running water. Rinse the meat, cut it into 3–4-cm/1¼-1½-inch pieces and season with salt and pepper. Heat 1 tablespoon of olive oil in a large frying pan over a medium-high heat, add the clam meat and sauté for 1–2 minutes until golden brown.

Divide the meat evenly between the shells and spoon the sauce over. Serve garnished with the strips of basil.

MUSSELS IN RED CURRY

STARTER, LUNCH — SERVES 4
PREPARATION 5 MINUTES — COOKING 10 MINUTES

You can of course buy red curry paste from your local store but I love to encourage you to make your own paste. It is easy to make from red, green or yellow chillies (chiles) and you can keep it in the fridge for 2–3 weeks.

INGREDIENTS

RED CURRY PASTE

1 onion, coarsely chopped
1 lemongrass stalk, coarse end cut off and stalk chopped into short lengths
4 garlic cloves
2-cm/¾-inch piece of fresh root ginger, peeled
3 red chillies (chiles), stalks removed
3 kaffir lime leaves, roughly chopped
handful of coriander (cilantro) leaves
½ tsp ground turmeric
1 tsp tomato purée (paste)
grated zest of 1 lime
3 tbsp sunflower oil
salt

MUSSELS

2 kg/4 lb 8 oz mussels in their shells, cleaned
300 ml/10 fl oz/1¼ cups coconut milk
4 spring onions (scallions), trimmed and finely sliced
½ red chilli (chile), sliced into thin rings
4 sprigs of coriander (cilantro), roughly chopped
1 lemongrass stalk, coarse end cut off and stalks roughly chopped
1 lime, cut in half

To make the red curry paste, put the onion, lemongrass, garlic, ginger, chillies (chiles), lime leaves, coriander (cilantro), turmeric, tomato purée (paste), lime zest, sunflower oil and a pinch of salt in a food processor and blitz to a coarse paste.

To cook the mussels, check the mussel shells are whole, discarding any that are broken. Heat a wok or large saucepan, add 2 tablespoons of the curry paste and fry for 1 minute. Add the coconut milk, whisk well and bring to the boil.

When the coconut milk comes to the boil, add the mussels and stir until coated in the milk. Cover the pan and cook the mussels for 5–7 minutes until the shells open, turning them over occasionally. When all the shells have opened, add half the spring onions (scallions), half the red chilli (chile) and coriander leaves and stir well.

Serve the mussels garnished with the remaining spring onions, chilli and coriander leaves, the chopped lemongrass stalk and lime halves to squeeze over.

TIP: any leftover curry paste can be kept in the refrigerator in a sealed container for up to 2 weeks.

PLATEAU DE FRUITS DE MER WITH ICE

MAIN COURSE — SERVES 4
PREPARATION 1 HOUR 25 MINUTES — COOKING 50 MINUTES

Fruits de mer is my earliest memory of fish. Every year whenever we went to France my parents would order a platter of the mixed seafood at a noisy restaurant in Paris. As a young boy, I was always amazed by the enormous piles of gnarled shells and the red and pink shellfish stacked on ice. According to the strict rules of French cuisine (the incomparable Larousse Gastronomique), a platter of fruits de mer should consist of: flat and round oysters, cockles, venus clams, short-neck (carpet shell) clams, mussels, scallops, periwinkles, whelks, prawns (shrimp), langoustines and perhaps half a North Sea crab or some sea urchins. But no one sticks to those rules today. Fruits de mer (literally, fruits of the sea) generally refers to any collection of molluscs, crustaceans and other small sea creatures, such as sea snails or sea urchins. Some are raw, some cooked, but everything is always eaten cold and served on a large platter or in a bowl with ice. Just pile on whatever you like best and can get fresh.

INGREDIENTS

4 litres/7 pints/17 cups of court bouillon (see page 392)
300 g/10 oz cockles in their shells
500 g/1 lb 2 oz mussels in their shells
200 g/7 oz periwinkles, in their shells
200 g/7 oz whelks, in their shells
500–600-g/1 lb 2-oz–1 lb 5-oz live lobster
700–800-g/1 lb 8-oz–1 lb 12-oz live crab
4 langoustines
2 kg/4 lb 8 oz crushed ice
8 large oysters, such as Creuses, Pacific or Japanese
8 Fines de Claire oysters
8 flat oysters such as Colchester Native or Olympia
300 g/10 oz king prawns (jumbo shrimp), cooked but not peeled
200 g/7 oz small prawns (shrimp), cooked but not peeled
4 lemons, cut in half
1 shallot, chopped
3 tbsp red wine vinegar
100 g/4 oz/scant ½ cup mayonnaise

Bring the court bouillon slowly to the boil and cook the shellfish in the following order, as they can make the bouillon cloudy.

First add the cockles to the bouillon, cook them for 3 minutes and then lift out with a slotted spoon and leave to cool. Add the mussels and cook until the shells have opened. Drain, discard any empty shells or ones that remain tightly closed and leave to cool. Cook the periwinkles for 3 minutes, drain and leave to cool. Render the lobster unconscious by putting it in the freezer for 1 hour. Remove the lobster and leave it for 15 minutes to come to room temperature. Cook the whelks for 8–12 minutes, depending on size, drain and leave to cool. Cook the lobster for 8 minutes in the bouillon, drain and rinse under cold running water. Cook the crab for 5–6 minutes, drain and leave to cool. Finally, add the langoustines to the bouillon, cook for 4–5 minutes, drain and leave to cool.

Cover a large platter with the crushed ice. Open all the oysters (see page 394) and arrange them over the ice. Add the rest of the seafood – cockles, mussels, periwinkles, whelks, lobster, crab, langoustines and both types of prawn (shrimp) – and tuck the lemon halves among them.

Mix the shallot with the red wine vinegar in a small bowl and serve alongside the platter of shellfish. Accompany with the mayonnaise, some good country bread and pins to extract the periwinkles from their shells.

NORMANDY MUSSELS

MAIN COURSE — SERVES 4
PREPARATION 10 MINUTES — COOKING 15 MINUTES

Before you start cooking mussels make sure you remove any that have broken shells and discard. If there are any that are open, tap them on the counter and if they close you can cook them, if not, throw them away. If you have cooked the mussels and they are open, they are ready to eat. If there are any that remain closed after cooking you should discard them.

INGREDIENTS

handful of flat-leaf parsley,
    stalks and leaves separated,
    and leaves finely chopped
60 g/2¼ oz/4 tbsp butter
2 shallots, chopped
2 garlic cloves, finely chopped
2 tbsp finely sliced celery
200 ml/7 fl oz/scant 1 cup
    white wine
4 kg/9 lb mussels in their shells,
    washed in plenty of cold water
3 tbsp double (heavy) cream
salt and pepper

Crush the parsley stalks with the blade of a heavy knife to bring out their flavour and then chop finely.

Heat the butter in a large pan over a medium-high heat. Add the shallots, garlic, celery and parsley stalks and fry for 2 minutes until the vegetables have softened, but not browned. Season to taste with some pepper.

Deglaze the pan with the wine and bring to the boil. Add the mussels and cover the pan with a lid. Cook, stirring the mussels occasionally to turn them over, until all the shells have opened. Lift the mussels from the pan with a slotted spoon, discarding any shells that are empty or have remained tightly closed.

Bring the mussel liquor to the boil and stir in the cream. Leave it to reduce over a low heat before returning the mussels to the pan. Stir well, cover and cook for a further 1 minute before stirring in three-quarters of the chopped parsley leaves.

Serve the mussels in a deep dish, garnished with the remaining chopped parsley. A green salad and white country bread make excellent accompaniments.

BLOODY MARY WITH OYSTERS

CANAPÉ — SERVES 4
PREPARATION 15 MINUTES

The Bloody Mary was invented in the 1920s or 30s, either in some upmarket speakeasy in New York City or a chic cocktail bar in Paris, but as to who actually invented it, no one knows. There are different accounts of how it got its name. The most popular is that the drink was named after England's Queen Mary I, who gained the sobriquet 'Bloody Mary' due to her relentless persecution of Protestants in the sixteenth century. There is a possible simpler explanation as well, which is that the cocktail was named after a waitress called Mary who worked at a bar known as the Bucket of Blood. Either way, a Bloody Mary is always a mix of vodka and tomato juice with perhaps salt, Tabasco and Worcestershire sauce added and served with a celery stick. In this recipe I've added oyster liquor to give a chic and complex brininess but, of course, if you don't want to add oyster juice to your Bloody Mary, you could add a little Bloody Mary to your oyster!

INGREDIENTS

8 oysters of your choice
200 ml/7 fl oz/scant 1 cup vodka
400 ml/14 fl oz/1 ¾ cups tomato juice
4 tbsp lemon juice
2 tsp Worcestershire sauce
Tabasco
ice cubes
4 celery sticks, with small tender leaves
salt and pepper
grated lemon zest, to garnish

Open the oysters with an oyster knife (see page 394) and loosen the meat from the shells, reserving the liquor. Strain the liquor to remove any fragments of shell.

Mix the vodka with the tomato juice and lemon juice. Add the oyster liquor and season to taste with the Worcestershire sauce, a few drops of Tabasco and black pepper. Taste and, if necessary, add a pinch of salt.

Three-quarters fill four tall (highball) glasses with ice cubes. Reserve 4 tablespoons of the vodka-tomato juice and pour the rest into the glasses. Add extra ice until the glasses are almost full and grind over a little extra pepper.

Trim the celery sticks so that they are taller than the glasses and stand one in each glass.

Serve the oysters in their shells topped with the reserved vodka-tomato juice, alongside the Bloody Marys. Sprinkle with a little pepper and lemon zest.

MUSSELS WITH BÉARNAISE SAUCE

CANAPÉ, STARTER — SERVES 4
PREPARATION 5 MINUTES — COOKING 20 MINUTES

Béarnaise sauce is a variation of Hollandaise and very traditional to serve with fish or shellfish. It's like making a warm mayonnaise, based on egg yolk with acidity. Where you use oil for mayonnaise, here you use clarified butter and add tarragon at the end. The creaminess of the sauce goes well with the saltiness of the mussels. Finger food at its finest.

INGREDIENTS

BÉARNAISE SAUCE

4 black peppercorns
1 shallot, chopped
2 tbsp finely chopped fresh
   tarragon, plus extra sprigs for
   garnish
3 tbsp red wine vinegar
3 egg yolks
125 g/4½ oz/9 tbsp clarified
   butter (see page 392)
salt and pepper

MUSSELS

25 g/1 oz/2 tbsp butter
1 white onion, chopped
1 garlic clove, finely chopped
100 ml/3½ fl oz/generous
   ⅓ cup white wine
2 kg/4 lb 8 oz mussels in their
   shells, cleaned
coarse sea salt for serving the
   mussels

To make the sauce, put the peppercorns, shallot and half the chopped tarragon with the red wine vinegar in a small saucepan and boil until reduced by two-thirds. Remove from the heat, strain and return to the pan.

To cook the mussels, heat the butter in a large pan over a medium heat and sauté the onion and garlic for 2 minutes without letting them brown. Deglaze with the white wine and add the mussels. Cover the pan and cook the mussels for 5–7 minutes, stirring occasionally. When the shells have opened, remove the mussels from the pan. Check if all the shells have opened and discard any empty shells or ones that have remained tightly closed.

Snap off the halves of the mussel shells with no meat in them and discard. Cover a large board or plank with coarse sea salt and press down the half shells with the mussels in them lightly into the salt.

To finish the sauce, briefly reheat the pan containing the strained tarragon vinegar mixture and then remove from the heat again. Whisk in the egg yolks thoroughly and return the pan to a low heat. Beat or whisk for 3 minutes and then gradually whisk in the clarified butter, a little at a time, without letting the sauce cook any more. Add the remaining tablespoon of chopped tarragon, season with salt and pepper and stir into the sauce.

Spoon the sauce over the mussel halves sitting on the coarse sea salt. Chop a few sprigs of tarragon and sprinkle over the mussels.

PERUVIAN-STYLE MUSSELS

STARTER, LUNCH — SERVES 4
PREPARATION **10 MINUTES** — COOKING **10 MINUTES**

When visiting Peru with my son, Bo, we ended up in a two-storey building in the lively district of Barranco in Lima. This dish was inspired by one in Isolina. It is a great way to eat chilled mussels with a chilled sauce. Just cook the mussels, chill down and add the wonderful salsa topping. If you like the heat from spice, leave the seeds in the fresh chilli (chile).

INGREDIENTS
MUSSELS

1 kg/2 lb 4 oz mussels
1 shallot, finely sliced
1 garlic clove, finely chopped
8 sprigs of coriander (cilantro), stalks and leaves separated and chopped
2 tbsp white wine
groundnut (peanut) oil for frying

TOPPING

1 red onion, finely diced
2 tomatoes, deseeded and finely diced
½ rocoto chilli (chile), also known as tree chilli (or another hot chilli such as habañero), deseeded and finely diced
1 garlic clove, finely chopped
2 tbsp corn kernels
grated zest and juice of 1 lime
1 tbsp extra virgin olive oil
1 lime, cut into wedges
salt and pepper

To cook the mussels, wash the mussels under cold running water and discard any with broken shells.

In a large pan, sauté the shallot, garlic and the coriander (cilantro) stalks in a dash of groundnut (peanut) oil over a medium-high heat until softened. Add the mussels and white wine, cover the pan and cook the mussels for 4–6 minutes until all the shells have opened.

Drain the mussels from the pan and discard any that have remained tightly closed. Snap off the half shells that contain the mussel meat and throw away the empty halves. Loosen the mussel meat from the shells with a small spoon or knife and then put each back in its half shell. Arrange the mussels in a single layer on a flat dish.

To prepare the topping, put the onion, tomatoes, chilli (chile), garlic and corn in a bowl and mix thoroughly. Add the lime juice, olive oil and chopped coriander (cilantro) leaves and season with salt and pepper.

Spoon the mixture on top of the mussels. Sprinkle over the lime zest and serve with lime wedges.

TIP: the mussels can be served on a bed of coarse sea salt or seaweed to prevent them sliding around. If using seaweed, it is important to boil it briefly first to kill any bacteria.

SEAWEED SALAD

STARTER, LUNCH — SERVES 4
PREPARATION **35 MINUTES** — COOKING **5 MINUTES**

Seaweed is becoming increasingly popular in Holland, which makes sense, as it is so healthy. Full of vitamins and minerals, it is also a great source of protein and would be an ideal way to both feed the world and reduce its meat consumption. Seaweed is full of flavour too, so it's no surprise that it has been on Asian menus for centuries. It is extremely rich in what the Japanese call umami: the fifth taste. Savoury is one way to describe it but from a scientific culinary angle, umami is the flavour of amino acids, in particular the amino acid MSG. In 1908, a Japanese chemist Kikunae Ikeda discovered that the white crystals on dried kombu (a type of seaweed) produced a savoury flavour that was quite distinct from the usual tastes of salty, sour, sweet and bitter. He called it umami, which means 'delicious' or 'delectable' in Japanese.

INGREDIENTS

DRESSING

3 tbsp soy sauce
3 tbsp lemon juice
1 tbsp orange juice
225 ml/7½ fl oz/scant 1 cup rice
  vinegar
1 tbsp mirin
1 tsp sesame oil
2-cm/¾-inch piece of fresh root
  ginger, peeled and grated
1 red chilli (chile), deseeded and
  very finely chopped
1 garlic clove, finely chopped

SALAD

450 g/1 lb different seaweeds
  of your choice – I'd suggest
  150 g/5 oz dried or fresh
  wakame seaweed, 150 g/5 oz
  dried or fresh seaweed threads
  and 150 g/5 oz dried or fresh
  bladderwrack
100 g/4 oz marsh samphire (sea
  asparagus/sea beans)
75 g/3 oz sea lavender
1 tbsp white sesame seeds,
  toasted

To make the dressing, whisk together the soy sauce, lemon juice, orange juice, rice vinegar, mirin and sesame oil. Add the ginger, chilli (chile) and garlic and set aside for 30 minutes to give the flavours time to develop.

To make the salad, first prepare the wakame, seaweed threads and bladderwrack. If using dried seaweeds, soak them in a bowl of warm water for 5 minutes. If using fresh seaweeds, dip them in a pan of boiling water for 10–15 seconds. Drain from the pan with a slotted spoon and immediately transfer them to a bowl of cold water with ice cubes added. Drain the different seaweeds and pat dry with kitchen paper (paper towels).

Blanch the marsh samphire (sea asparagus/sea beans) and sea lavender in a pan of unsalted boiling water for 30 seconds. Drain from the pan with a slotted spoon and transfer immediately to a bowl of iced water to cool. Drain the vegetables and pat dry with kitchen paper.

Mix the dressing with the different sea vegetables and sprinkle with the sesame seeds.

WASHINGTON D.C.

NEW ORLEANS

UNITED STATES
BLUE CRAB & SALMON

NEW ORLEANS, UNITED STATES — 30°16'30.7"N 89°46'52.2"W

FAO 31 ATLANTIC OCEAN W

ROY & MITCH

BLUE SWIMMER CRABS IN ALLIGATOR COUNTRY

—✦—

The swampy delta of Louisiana is real alligator country. Take a boat down the bayous and it's like being in the James Bond movie 'Live and Let Die'. Alligators could be lurking anywhere among the lush vegetation along the river banks, although the waters contain even more crabs than alligators, and not just any kind of crab – this is where you can find the delicious blue swimmer crab.

These crabs have made their way from the Gulf of Mexico to lay their eggs in the salt water of the swamps. Their eggs drift on the tidal currents to the delta's nutrient-rich, brackish water where the tiny crabs grow until they are large enough to return to the sea to reproduce. The delta is more like a system of lagoons, one of the largest being Lake Ponchartrain near New Orleans. The lake, crossed by two bridges, one carrying a highway and the other a rusty railway bridge, is home to the best crabs.

As many as 2,400 crab fishermen actively work Lake Ponchartrain. They always fish in pairs in two-man boats, such as Mitch and Roy. They sail the lake every day to retrieve their catch and set their traps out again, covering a vast area in the process. Captain Roy steers, connecting the buoys to an electric winch to retrieve the traps, while Mitch is busy pulling the traps aboard at the rear end of the boat, which he empties and throws back into the sea. He has to do this very quickly, as the boat is still moving forward at a steady pace.

They may not be as dangerous as alligators but still, you have to treat swimmer crabs with care. They tend to be quite aggressive and agile – they seem to be able to snap at your fingers no matter how you approach them. The only way to keep your fingers safe is to grab them at the back between their swimming legs and hold them between your thumb and index finger. That's why Mitch likes to empty the traps into a container of icy water as a minute in the water will stun them briefly.

After this the crabs are sorted by sex into the blue males and females with red claws, and are placed in wooden crates. The crates are not at all practical, they are just part and parcel of the whole tradition. When the crates are full, they are covered with wet jute sacks, which not only keep the crabs inside moist, they are also heavy enough to ensure the crabs stay in the crates.

Most of the fishermen are from families that have been fishing for crabs for generations. They originally used hand lines and then later nets, but since the 1970s they have employed traps. This is much better for sustainability than dragging nets along the bottom, because there is hardly any bycatch. The crab traps are fitted with escape rings, which allow the smaller crabs measuring less than 15 cm/6 inches to escape. It is also mandatory to release immature female crabs over 15 cm/6 inches and, as a result, all the crabs in Lake Ponchartrain are MSC-certified. Only the small quantity that are part of the bycatch from prawn (shrimp) fishing – due to the use of drag nets – are not certified.

Back on the dockside, Mitch and Roy drag their crates onto weighing scales that are set into recesses in the wooden piers. Some of the catch is sold fresh, the remainder is steamed under pressure that same night and then sent to the cannery across the road the following day. The cooked crabs are passed around from table to table on large blue trays. First, the jumbo lump meat, from the large muscle that controls the crab's paddle fins, is removed. Next, they take the ordinary lump meat from the walking legs and then the meat from the arms. It is all packed into small jars and sold fresh, pasteurized or frozen. The claws are prepared as an appetizer to serve with drinks, the shell on the tip of each claw being left on so the appetizer comes with its own toothpick.

Blue swimmer crabmeat is delicate, rich and sweet, with a vanilla-like flavour and a firm and juicy texture. Regarded as a great delicacy, they are very popular across the United States, from the west coast to New England. Blue swimmer crabs are often served whole but they are also perfect for making a traditional Louisiana Seafood Gumbo (see page 322).

CRAB COCKTAIL

STARTER, LUNCH — SERVES 4
PREPARATION 15 MINUTES

The traditional crab cocktail is based on a whiskey sauce but for this recipe I made it slightly different because I wanted to show off the true fresh flavour of crabmeat with fennel, orange, lettuce and radish. My advice when making a seafood cocktail is not to be too generous with mayonnaise – let the fish be the hero. The crab could be easily substituted with crayfish or prawns (shrimp).

INGREDIENTS

4 tbsp mayonnaise
finely grated zest and juice of
   ½ lime
100 ml/3½ fl oz/generous
   ⅓ cup orange juice
300 g/10 oz white crabmeat
1 (or 2) Little Gem (baby cos/
   baby romaine) lettuces
12 orange segments
½ fennel bulb, thinly sliced
4 radishes, thinly sliced
cayenne pepper
salt and pepper

Mix the mayonnaise with the lime juice and orange juice. Add the crab and season with salt and pepper. Set aside.

Separate the lettuces into leaves, wash them under cold running water and pat dry with kitchen paper (paper towels).

Arrange a couple of lettuce leaves in each of four cocktail glasses or glass dessert bowls and spoon the crab mayonnaise on top. Add the orange segments, fennel slices and radish slices. Dust with a little cayenne pepper and sprinkle with the lime zest. Serve with good country bread or toast.

SEAFOOD GUMBO

STARTER, LUNCH — SERVES 6
PREPARATION 10 MINUTES — COOKING 1 HOUR 15 MINUTES

The best-known dish of Louisiana, we enjoyed this combination of meat and fish mixed with a local roux. They say the roux is the soul of the gumbo where they combine flour and oil instead of butter so that you can reach a colour between peanut butter and chocolate over a long cooking time and butter would burn long before it was ready. It's a meat and fish dish so alongside the crab you add prawns (shrimp) and smoked sausage.

INGREDIENTS

250 g/9 oz/1 cup long-grain rice
250 ml/8 fl oz/1 cup groundnut (peanut) oil
250 g/9 oz/1¾ cups plain (all-purpose) flour
1 onion, roughly chopped
1 green (bell) pepper, deseeded and roughly chopped
1 orange (bell) pepper, deseeded and roughly chopped
3 celery sticks, cut into 1-cm/½-inch pieces
2 garlic cloves, finely chopped
1 litre/1¾ pints/4¼ cups fish stock (see page 390)
250 g/9 oz okra (or green/French beans if okra is not available)
3 large tomatoes, deseeded and chopped
150 g/5 oz smoked sausage, roughly chopped
12 large raw prawns (shrimp), unpeeled
400 g/14 oz white crabmeat, broken into chunks
10 sprigs of flat-leaf parsley, roughly chopped
cayenne pepper
salt and pepper

Put the rice in a saucepan and add enough cold water to cover the rice by about 1 cm/½ inch. Bring to the boil, lower the heat and cover the pan. Simmer the rice gently for 10 minutes and then take the pan off the heat without removing the lid.

Put the oil and flour in a large cast-iron, or other heavy, pan and stir or whisk until smooth. Stir over the heat for 10–15 minutes until the roux darkens in colour to a shade between peanut butter and chocolate. Add the onion, green (bell) pepper, orange (bell) pepper, celery and garlic and cook gently for a couple of minutes until all the vegetables have softened. Pour in the fish stock, cover the pan and lower the heat.

Remove the lid from the pan after 15 minutes and add the okra, tomatoes, chunks of sausage, prawns (shrimp) and crab. Put the lid back on the pan and leave the seafood gumbo over a low heat for 30 minutes.

Remove the lid again and stir in the parsley. Season with a pinch of cayenne and salt and pepper to taste. Finally add the cooked rice to the soup and stir well before serving.

CRAB & PUMPKIN CANNELLONI

MAIN COURSE — SERVES 4
PREPARATION **10 MINUTES** — COOKING **1 HOUR 10 MINUTES**

Crab and lobster traps sometimes break loose from their buoys and get lost on the seabed, but any creatures caught inside are not doomed to remain there for eternity. A lobster trap is held together with iron clamps that will rust away if left under water for any length of time. Similarly, a crab trap is made of cotton cords that gradually disintegrate, so both traps collapse and set their captives free. To prevent adult lobsters killing younger ones in the trap, openings allow the smaller ones to crawl out into the open sea. Young crabs can work their way out between the cotton cords of the traps.

INGREDIENTS
FILLING

1 small pumpkin (or squash),
   deseeded, peeled, halved and
   chopped into chunks
2 garlic cloves, crushed
handful of fresh thyme,
   chopped plus a few sprigs for
   garnish
400 g/14 oz white crab meat
   (fresh, frozen or canned)
4 dried lasagne sheets
100 g/4 oz Parmesan cheese,
   grated

BÉCHAMEL SAUCE

50 g/2 oz/4 tbsp butter
4 tbsp plain (all-purpose) flour
500 ml/18 fl oz/2 cups milk
100 ml/3½ fl oz/generous
   ⅓ cup tomato juice
salt and pepper
olive oil for drizzling and frying

ALTERNATIVE SHELLFISH

lobster

Preheat the oven to 180°C/350°F/Gas Mark 4.

Spread out the chunks of pumpkin on a baking sheet lined with baking parchment (baking paper) and drizzle with olive oil. Roast in the oven for 30–40 minutes or until the pumpkin is tender. Leave to cool.

To make the béchamel sauce, melt the butter in a saucepan over a low heat. Stir in the flour off the heat until smooth. Return to the heat and cook for about 1 minute, stirring with a spatula and not letting the mixture brown. Gradually whisk in the milk and season with salt and pepper. Stir in the tomato juice and heat until the sauce is thickened and smooth – if it becomes too thick, stir in some extra milk.

To assemble the cannelloni, chop the pumpkin into small pieces. Heat 1 tablespoon of olive oil in a frying pan (skillet) and fry the garlic and chopped thyme for 1 minute. Add the crab and pumpkin and heat through for a few minutes.

Meanwhile, cook the lasagne sheets in a large pan of lightly salted boiling water for about 8 minutes or until they are al dente. Drain from the pan with a slotted spoon to a colander and rinse lightly under cold running water.

Cover the base of an ovenproof dish with a thin layer of béchamel sauce. Divide the crab and pumpkin mixture between the lasagne sheets and roll the sheets around the filling to make even-size rolls. Lay the rolls in the dish and spoon over the remaining béchamel sauce. Scatter over the Parmesan and bake the cannelloni in the oven for 10–15 minutes until the top is golden brown.

Serve garnished with a few thyme sprigs.

CRAB CAKES
WITH LEMON MAYONNAISE

CANAPÉ, STARTER, LUNCH — SERVES 4
PREPARATION **2 HOURS 20 MINUTES** — COOKING **10 MINUTES**

Old Bay spice blend is used for crab cakes and is worth seeking out but by no means essential. Here I recommend a combination of fresh herbs to achieve the perfect taste. When mixing the ingredients together to form the patties, keep it chunky for added bite.

INGREDIENTS

CRAB CAKES (MAKES ABOUT 8)

400 g/14 oz white crab meat (fresh, frozen, or canned)
2–3 tbsp mayonnaise
1 tbsp Dijon mustard
1 egg, beaten
1 tsp smoked paprika
freshly grated nutmeg
juice of 1/4 lemon
1 tsp Worcestershire sauce
4 tbsp panko or dry breadcrumbs
handful of flat-leaf parsley, finely chopped
8 chives, finely chopped
1 lemon, cut into wedges
groundnut (peanut) oil for frying
salt and pepper

LEMON MAYONNAISE

8 tbsp mayonnaise
finely grated zest and juice of 1 lemon
salt and pepper

To make the crab cakes, drain the crabmeat thoroughly and pat dry with kitchen paper (paper towels).

Whisk the mayonnaise, mustard and egg together in a bowl and stir in the paprika, a little nutmeg, the lemon juice and Worcestershire sauce. Add the crab and knead or mash everything together without making the mixture too smooth.

Stir in the panko, parsley and chives and season with salt and pepper to taste. Mix again and then use your hands to shape the mixture into small, round flat cakes, adding a little extra panko if the cakes still feel rather wet. Place the crab cakes on a plate, cover with cling film (plastic wrap) and chill in the refrigerator for 2 hours.

To make the lemon mayonnaise, mix together the mayonnaise, lemon zest and juice. Season with salt and pepper.

Heat some groundnut (peanut) oil for shallow-frying in a frying pan (skillet) and fry the crab cakes over a medium-high heat for 4–5 minutes on each side until browned. Drain onto a plate lined with kitchen paper.

Serve the crab cakes with the lemon mayonnaise and lemon wedges to squeeze over. Sprinkle with a little extra lemon zest, if wished.

Pontchartrain Blue Crab, Inc.
MSC TRAP CAUGHT
Roy S.

Name	1's	M/M	Fem	Fac
			10	

AVOCADO & SWEET POTATO SALAD WITH CRAB

STARTER, LUNCH — SERVES 4
PREPARATION 15 MINUTES — COOKING 15 MINUTES

In homage to the beautiful Mexican people working at the fishery in Slidell I made this guacamole-inspired salad for them. The fresh flavours of the onion and tomato, the creaminess of the avocado and sweet potato, and the beautiful flavour of the crab was my way to thank them for a wonderful stay.

INGREDIENTS

1 large sweet potato
20 cherry tomatoes
1 red onion, thinly sliced
1 red chilli (chile), deseeded and thinly sliced
1 green chilli (chile), deseeded and thinly sliced
2 avocados, peeled, pitted and diced
finely grated zest and juice of 1 lime
300 g/10 oz white crabmeat (freshly cooked if possible)
2 tbsp extra virgin olive oil
leaves of 8 coriander (cilantro) sprigs
salt and pepper

Boil the sweet potato in a pan of lightly salted water for about 15 minutes until tender. Drain, leave to cool, then peel the sweet potato and cut it into approximately 1-cm/½-inch cubes.

Quarter the cherry tomatoes and scoop or cut out the seeds. Put the tomatoes in a large bowl and add the onion, chillies (chiles) and avocados.

Stir in the lime juice, followed by the crabmeat. If the crabmeat is not too cold it will taste better. Stir in the olive oil and most of the coriander (cilantro) leaves, reserving a few leaves for garnish.

Season to taste with salt and pepper and serve garnished with the remaining coriander.

STUFFED CRAB

STARTER, LUNCH — SERVES 4
PREPARATION 20 MINUTES — COOKING 10 MINUTES

There are many variations of crab and here we use the brown crab, which can be found around the waters of the UK, Netherlands and Belgium as well as many other regions. They are fantastic to stuff. Stuffing crab means to extract the wonderful crabmeat, mix it with other ingredients and give it back to the shell before serving.

INGREDIENTS

4 fresh live brown crabs
8 tomatoes, deseeded and cut into small cubes
4 hard-boiled (hard-cooked) eggs, peeled in finely chopped
2 celery stalks, cut into small cubes
2 red onions, finely chopped
2 tbsp finely chopped parsley leaves
8 tbsp panko breadcrumbs
8 tbsp Parmesan cheese
40 g/3 tbsp unsalted butter, cut into cubes
lemon zest, to serve
salt and pepper

Preheat the oven to 200°C/400°F/Gas Mark 6.

Cook the live crabs in a large pot of boiling water or fish stock for 6 minutes. You may need to do this in batches depending on the size of your pot.

Lift the cooked crabs from the pan and take off the claws. Extract the crabmeat from the claws and set it aside.

Open the crab body from the underneath and empty the shell of meat, adding it to the claw meat. Clean the crab shells under cold running water and set aside.

Mix the crabmeat, tomatoes, egg, celery, red onion and parsley together. Season with salt and pepper, then use the mixture to stuff the cleaned crab shells.

Mix the panko breadcrumbs with the Parmesan cheese and sprinkle over the crab opening.

Divide the butter equally between the crabs and put on top of the breadcrumb mixture.

Bake the stuffed crabs in the preheated oven for 4–5 minutes until nicely caramelized on top.

Serve the crabs with lemon zest sprinkled on top.

SALMON

—⤳—

While we didn't make a special trip to Alaska, no fish cookbook would be complete without salmon. Norway and Scotland are famous for their salmon but the Norwegian and Scottish salmon sold in shops are almost invariably farmed. Today, there's not much wild salmon left in the Atlantic, but at one time it swam in almost every European river from Scandinavia and the Baltic states, to France and even Spain. As salmon swim all the way up river to spawn each year, the construction of dams and sluice gates in the eighteenth and nineteenth centuries started a significant decline in their numbers. The end for Atlantic salmon came in the 1950s, however, when the Danes discovered that all Atlantic salmon, including those that spawned in the rivers of the east coast of Canada and America, came together at one place off Greenland. Once vessels arrived to fish there, it was soon over.

Farmed salmon is a useful product as it's possible to adjust its colour and fat content to meet demand by changing the salmon's diet. Wild salmon should always be frozen, smoked or cooked at over 60°C/140°F to kill any possible parasites. This isn't necessary with farmed salmon, which makes it ideal for sushi. Nevertheless, wild salmon still has the finer flavour. These days wild salmon always comes from the Pacific Ocean and the best is from Alaska. There are two reasons for this. Firstly they have the most sustainable regulations and, secondly, the longest and steepest rivers.

To spawn, salmon always swim back from the sea to the place up river where they were born, swimming against the flow all the way. Once the salmon leave the sea and begin swimming upstream they stop eating and have to rely on the reserves of fat they have built up to get them up the river. It's best therefore to catch them at the start of their journey in the estuary when they are at their fattest. Salmon born in the Yukon, the longest river, and the Copper River, the river with the steepest gradient, have the longest and hardest journeys. Of all Alaska's salmon they are the fattest and have the fullest flavour.

Alaska's state legislature has imposed strict sustainability regulations. There are five types of salmon in the Pacific and, during the salmon season, biologists from the Department of Fish and Game set quotas every day as to how many salmon of each type can be caught in each of Alaska's rivers. They set the quota by counting the number of salmon that arrive at the estuaries, using sonar equipment.

One of the finest fisheries in Alaska is the Kwik'Pak salmon fishery in the village of Emmonak, not far from the mouth of the Yukon. Northwest Alaska is isolated and thinly populated, so there are not many roads and people tend to travel by light aircraft. It's also one of the poorest regions of the United States populated by the original inhabitants, Yup'ik Eskimos. The Yup'ik still survive the winter mainly by eating the salmon they smoke in the summer, but life has improved as commercial salmon fishing has taken hold. It means they can continue fishing and maintain not just a sustainable fish stock but their own traditional community as well.

DILL-CURED GRAVLAX WITH MUSTARD

STARTER, LUNCH — SERVES 4
PREPARATION 12 HOURS 15 MINUTES

The 'grav' of gravlax means 'trench' in Swedish and is to literally to keep underground. In older times you would cure the salmon underground but this is by no means necessary. Now, curing underground is only done to add flavour.

INGREDIENTS

GRAVLAX

1 side of salmon fillet weighing about 800 g/1 lb 12 oz, skin left on
2 tbsp coriander seeds
2 tbsp fennel seeds
1 tsp peppercorns
4 tbsp coarse sea salt
3 tbsp granulated sugar
3 tbsp vodka
finely grated zest of 1 lemon
finely grated zest of 1 orange
handful of dill sprigs, roughly chopped
2 tbsp roughly chopped flat-leaf parsley
1 lemon, cut into wedges

MUSTARD & DILL SAUCE

8 tbsp olive oil
2 tbsp Dijon mustard
handful of dill sprigs, finely chopped
1 tbsp honey
juice of 1 lemon
salt and pepper

To prepare the gravlax, lay the salmon, skin-side up, on a large board and cut slashes in the skin with a sharp knife, 5 cm/2 inches apart, 2 cm/³/₄ inch long and 1 cm/¹/₂ deep, to expose the flesh of the fish. This will allow the liquid that is released while the fish is marinating to flow out. Turn the salmon over and check for any remaining bones, removing these with tweezers. Cover a baking sheet with a large sheet of cling film (plastic wrap), letting it overhang the sides of the sheet. Lift the salmon, skin-side down, onto the baking sheet.

Coarsely crush half the coriander and fennel seeds and all the peppercorns in a mortar. Add the salt, sugar, vodka, lemon zest, orange zest, half the dill and all the parsley and crush everything together in the mortar until fine.

Spread the mixture evenly over the salmon flesh and wrap the cling film around the fish, pressing out the air. Place another baking sheet on top of the salmon and weigh it down with several heavy food jars or cans. Chill the fish in the refrigerator for 8–12 hours.

Remove the cling film from the salmon and carefully scrape off the marinade with your fingers, taking care not to damage the flesh. Rinse the fish carefully under cold running water to remove the salt and spice granules. Don't worry about being too thorough as it's sufficient just to remove the coarse layer. Pat the fillet dry with kitchen paper (paper towels).

Crush the remaining fennel and coriander seeds roughly in the mortar. Mix with the remaining chopped dill and sprinkle over the salmon. Press the herb mixture gently onto the flesh of the fish with your hands.

To make the sauce, mix together the olive oil, mustard, dill, honey and lemon juice in a bowl and season to taste with salt and pepper.

Starting at the tail end, cut the fish into thin, diagonal slices using a sharp carving knife.

Serve the gravlax with the mustard and dill sauce and accompany with country bread or toast and lemon wedges.

SCRAMBLED EGGS WITH SMOKED SALMON & SALMON ROE

BREAKFAST, LUNCH — SERVES 4
PREPARATION 5 MINUTES — COOKING 10 MINUTES

The Kwik'Pak salmon farm lies in the Yukon estuary in northwest Alaska. Yup'ik Eskimos fish there for the finest salmon, just as the fish are about to start their migration to the source of the river, where they head each summer to spawn. The female fish are full of roe by that time. When Yup'iks fish for salmon, the whole family gets involved, even the smaller children if their grandmother can't look after them at home. They are carried on the backs of the grownups, if necessary. Teenagers under sixteen aren't legally allowed on the water alone, so they work in the harbour in a special section called the nursery, where the salmon eggs are collected. After the eggs have been washed they are brined for 10 minutes in salt water and then left to drain. The shelves of plastic trays full of shiny bright orange pearls are a really magnificent sight and the eggs are delicious to eat. Fresh, salty and oily, they pop in your mouth in small explosions of flavour. They are always a treat whether you enjoy them for lunch, dinner or even breakfast, spooned on top of scrambled egg.

INGREDIENTS

4 slices of bread
8 eggs
4 tsp milk
20 g/¾ oz/1½ tbsp butter
200 g/7 oz smoked salmon, chopped
25 g/1 oz salmon roe
4 chives, finely chopped
salt and pepper

Toast the slices of bread in a toaster or under the grill (broiler).

Beat the eggs and milk together with a fork and season with salt and pepper.

Heat the butter in a frying pan (skillet) over a low heat. Pour the egg mixture into the pan and stir with a wooden spoon. Stop stirring every 10 seconds for 10 seconds so the eggs set slowly. Add the pieces of salmon and half the chives when the eggs are almost set and cook for a further 1 minute.

Spoon the scrambled eggs evenly over the slices of toast and serve garnished with the salmon roe and the remaining chives. Finally, grind over some pepper.

CLUB SANDWICH WITH SMOKED SOCKEYE SALMON

LUNCH — SERVES 4
PREPARATION 10 MINUTES — COOKING 5 MINUTES

Five varieties of wild salmon are found in the Pacific, each slightly different in appearance and flavour. They often go by two different names – a local name and an English one. Chinook or king salmon is by far the largest and therefore the most highly prized. Coho (or silver) and Pink varieties are smaller and excellent for frying, while Keta, also known as chum, is usually reserved for canning, although it is plump and delicious to eat fresh. Sockeye salmon is different from all the others as its flesh is not pink but deep red. Sockeye is the only salmon that doesn't prey on other fish, eating plankton and tiny prawns (shrimp). This accounts for its colour, which deepens when the fish is smoked.

INGREDIENTS

12 thick slices of bread
175 ml/6 fl oz/¾ cup mayonnaise
finely grated zest and juice of 1 lemon
2 avocados
½ lettuce, washed and leaves separated
400 g/14 oz smoked sockeye (or farmed) salmon, cut into small slices
2 tbsp capers
½ cucumber, sliced
1 red onion, finely sliced
salt and pepper

Toast the slices of bread in a toaster or under the grill (broiler) until golden-brown.

Mix the mayonnaise with the lemon zest and most of the juice, reserving some of the juice to spoon over the avocados to prevent them discolouring. Season to taste with salt and pepper.

Cut the avocados in half, remove the stones (pits), spoon out the flesh and cut into slices. Sprinkle with the reserved lemon juice.

Have the remaining ingredients ready to build the sandwiches.

Spread one slice of toast with a spoonful of lemon mayonnaise and cover with a few lettuce leaves, followed by a slice of smoked salmon. Grind over some pepper. Continue by adding capers, a slice of avocado, cucumber slices and red onion slices. Spread mayonnaise on both sides of the next slice of toast, place on top and repeat the layers, starting with the lettuce leaves. The third slice of toast should be spread with mayonnaise only on the underside before you place it on top of the sandwich.

Make three more sandwiches in the same way with the remaining slices of toast and filling ingredients, reserving four slices of smoked salmon.

Cut each sandwich in half and and pile the halves on top of each other with the remaining slices of salmon between. Skewer the stacks to keep the club sandwiches upright and serve.

SALMON, TUNA & PRAWN (SHRIMP) PANCAKE

STARTER, LUNCH — SERVES 4
PREPARATION **30 MINUTES** — COOKING **20 MINUTES**

Smoked or pre-cooked prawns (shrimp) are often served as canapés and for this tart of pancake layers combines them with egg, smoked fish and tuna. Serve it as a slice or small bite-size pieces.

INGREDIENTS

BATTER (TO MAKE 5 PANCAKES)

250 g/9 oz/1¾ cups plain (all-purpose) flour
3 eggs
500 ml/18 fl oz/2 cups milk
butter for frying

EGG SALAD

3 eggs
½ tsp paprika
½ tsp curry powder
3 tbsp mayonnaise

TUNA

1 x 160-g (5½-oz) can of skip-jack tuna, well drained
1 onion, finely chopped
1 tbsp capers
2 tbsp mayonnaise

PRAWN (SHRIMP) & AVOCADO

2 avocados, peeled and pitted
juice of ½ lemon
200 g/7 oz small prawns (shrimp), peeled
4 chives, finely chopped

SALMON

300 g/10 oz smoked sockeye (or farmed) salmon, cut into small pieces
1 lemon, cut into wedges
salt and pepper

To make the batter, sift the flour into a large bowl. To avoid any lumps forming, first whisk the eggs into the flour and then gradually whisk or stir in the milk, a little at a time, until you have a smooth batter. Season with a pinch of salt.

Heat a little butter in a frying pan (skillet) and, when foaming, pour in one-fifth of the batter. Swirl the pan so the batter coats the base evenly and fry until golden underneath. Flip the pancake over to cook the other side. Remove from the pan and cook four more pancakes in the same way using the remaining batter and adding more butter to the pan, as necessary. Allow the pancakes to cool at room temperature.

Bring a pan of water to the boil and cook the eggs for 8 minutes. Drain and cool under cold running water. Peel the eggs and mash them with a fork. Mix with the paprika, curry powder and mayonnaise. Season with salt and pepper.

Flake the tuna into a bowl and stir in the onion, capers and mayonnaise. Season with salt and pepper.

Cut the avocado flesh into small dice and drizzle with the lemon juice to prevent discolouration. Mix carefully with the prawns (shrimp) and chives so the avocado flesh doesn't break up. Season with salt and pepper.

Now begin to stack. Lay a pancake on a large plate and top with the tuna salad. Lay the next pancake on top and cover with half the smoked salmon. Add another pancake and cover with the egg salad, followed by the fourth pancake and remaining salmon. Add the final pancake and cover with the avocado, prawns and chives.

Cut the pancake stack into wedges with a sharp knife and serve with the lemon wedges to squeeze over.

SALMON TERIYAKI

MAIN COURSE — SERVES 4
PREPARATION 10 MINUTES — COOKING 15 MINUTES

Teriyaki is a traditional sweet Japanese sauce, based on a mixture of soy sauce, sugar and mirin (rice wine). The sauce is used to coat chicken, meat or fish for frying or grilling (broiling) and adds a delicious flavour as well as a lovely shiny glaze. In Japanese yaki means 'cooked over direct heat' (for example grilled/broiled or fried) and teri refers to a shine or lustre. When you fry salmon coated with teriyaki sauce, take care not to let the high sugar content burn the fish.

INGREDIENTS
TERIYAKI SAUCE
175 ml/6 fl oz/¾ cup sake
3 tbsp soy sauce
1 tbsp honey
½ tbsp balsamic vinegar
25 g/1 oz sugar

SALAD
3 tbsp white sesame seeds
16 radishes, cut into thin strips
4 spring onions (scallions), trimmed and cut into 4-cm/1½-inch lengths
juice of 1 lemon
handful of coriander (cilantro) leaves, coarsely chopped
4 x 150–175 g/5–6 oz salmon fillets, skinned
groundnut (peanut) oil, for frying
salt and pepper

To make the teriyaki sauce, put all the ingredients in a saucepan and stir over a low heat until the sugar has dissolved. Leave the sauce to bubble over the heat until it has reduced by two-thirds and thickened slightly.

To make the salad, toast the sesame seeds in a dry frying pan (skillet) for about 1 minute until the seeds are golden brown. Remove from the pan and set aside to cool.

Mix together the radishes, spring onions (scallions), lemon juice, coriander (cilantro) and 2 tablespoons of the sesame seeds in a bowl. Season with salt and pepper.

To cook the salmon, heat 2 tablespoons of groundnut (peanut) oil in a frying pan (skillet) over a high heat. Add the salmon to the pan and fry for 1 minute. Turn the heat down to medium-high and, depending on the thickness of the fish, turn the fillets over after 2–3 minutes. Brush the tops of the fillets with some of the teriyaki sauce. Turn the salmon over after 1 minute and fry the other side for another minute. Brush with teriyaki sauce, so both sides are covered. Turn the salmon over again and fry for another 30 seconds.

Divide the salad between four serving plates and place the salmon fillets on top. Sprinkle with the remaining sesame seeds.

ASPARAGUS WITH HOT SMOKED SALMON

LUNCH, MAIN COURSE — SERVES 4
PREPARATION **10 MINUTES** — COOKING **30 MINUTES**

Dried fish can be kept for a long time as micro-organisms cannot develop without water and therefore the fish doesn't rot. In cold climates people used to hang fish in the open air to dry, but in temperate, humid climates the fish began to rot before they were completely dry. To remedy this the fish was brined first so that the salt could remove any liquid in the fish and destroy any mould. But even that was not always enough as fatty fish, in particular, were prone to oxidize, producing a rancid flavour. To speed up the process, the fish would be hung near a fire. Where there's fire, there's smoke, and it was discovered that smoke preserved fresh foods. It contains hundreds of different elements, some of which kill micro-organisms or stop them growing and slow the oxidization of fat, while others give the fish an exquisitely smoky flavour. In fact, that delicious flavour is really the only reason we still smoke fish today! If the smoke is cold, the fish is known as cold-smoked and that's the sort you eat on your thinly-sliced brown bread and butter or on crackers. In this recipe we use hot-smoked salmon, where the fish is already cooked by the hot smoke.

INGREDIENTS

1 kg/2 lb 4 oz white asparagus
500 g/1 lb 2 oz baby new
  potatoes, skins on
2 eggs
500 g/1 lb 2 oz hot-smoked
  salmon fillet
250 g/9 oz clarified butter (see
  page 392)
handful of flat-leaf parsley,
  finely chopped
salt and pepper

Preheat the oven to 160°C/325°F/Gas Mark 3.

Shave the asparagus spears (stalks) with a vegetable peeler, making sure you run the peeler twice down the length of each to remove any hard bumps. Trim 1 cm/½ inch off the base of each spear. Put the asparagus in a large saucepan of cold water, add a pinch of salt and bring the water to the boil. Turn off the heat once it has boiled and cover the pan. Leave for 15 minutes by which time the asparagus will be tender.

Meanwhile, bring another pan of lightly salted water to the boil, add the baby potatoes and cook for 10–15 minutes until the potatoes are tender. Drain and keep them warm in the pan, covered with a lid.

Cook the eggs in a pan of boiling water for 6 minutes while the asparagus and potatoes are cooking, by which time the yolks should still be slightly 'runny'. Drain, cool the eggs under cold running water and then peel and cut them in half. Lift the asparagus out of their water using a slotted spoon.

Warm the smoked salmon in the oven for 5 minutes. Heat the butter in a pan until melted and stir in the parsley.

Remove the skin from the salmon and break the flesh into pieces. Halve the potatoes and add to the butter and parsley with the asparagus. Season with salt and pepper.

Divide the potatoes, asparagus and salmon between four serving plates, spoon over the buttery juices and place half a boiled (cooked) egg on top.

SALMON LASAGNE WITH CAPERS & DILL

MAIN COURSE — SERVES 4
PREPARATION **25 MINUTES** — COOKING **40 MINUTES**

One of the beautiful things about the salmon is that the life of a salmon starts up river and then it finds a way to the salty water of the ocean. There it feeds itself for 4–5 years before returning to precisely the same spot where it was born to spawn its own eggs. It is the beautiful story of wild salmon and Alaska is famous for protecting that natural journey. Only when enough salmon has swum up river to guarantee the population for the next season do they start fishing.

INGREDIENTS

about 700 g/I lb 8 oz salmon
    fillet, skinned
2 tbsp capers
handful of fresh dill sprigs,
    finely chopped
2 tbsp white wine
I leek, trimmed, green parts
    removed and thinly sliced
50 g/2 oz/4 tbsp butter
4 tbsp plain (all-purpose) flour
500 ml/I lb 2 oz/2 cups milk
9 dried lasagne sheets
150 g/5 oz Parmesan cheese,
    grated
freshly grated nutmeg
olive oil for drizzling and frying
salt and pepper

ALTERNATIVE FISH

cod or haddock

Preheat the oven to 180°C/350°F/Gas Mark 4.

Put the salmon in an ovenproof dish, drizzle with olive oil and add the capers, dill and white wine. Bake the salmon in the oven for 8 minutes and then leave to cool. Flake the salmon into small pieces and mix with the capers and dill.

Heat I tablespoon of olive oil in a frying pan (skillet) over a medium-high heat, add the leek and I tablespoon of water and cook the leek until it is tender.

Melt the butter in a saucepan over a low heat. Take the pan off the heat and stir in the flour. Cook for I minute without letting the roux brown, stirring with a spatula. Gradually whisk in the milk, season with nutmeg, salt and pepper and continue to whisk until the sauce is thickened and smooth.

Cover the base of a greased shallow ovenproof dish with a thin layer of the sauce and lay three lasagne sheets on top. Spoon another layer of sauce over the lasagne sheets and cover with a layer of salmon and leeks. Add more lasagne sheets, salmon and leeks and sauce, repeating the layers until the dish is filled and finishing with lasagne sheets and a layer of sauce – the sauce should completely cover the lasagne. Sprinkle the grated cheese on top.

Bake the lasagne in the oven for 25–30 minutes until golden brown and bubbling. Serve directly from the dish.

MARKETS

FRESHLY CAUGHT, BOUGHT FISH

FISH MARKETS ARE ALWAYS BUSTLING

— ⋊═ —

In compiling this book we have travelled to some of the most authentic and sustainable fisheries. We selected them because they set a perfect example for the future and give a diverse picture of the different types of certified sustainable fisheries around the world. Naturally, there are many other fisheries that behave responsibly and other types of fish that are sustainably caught elsewhere in the world. We wanted to cook with those, too, and to buy them we went to markets.

Good fish markets are always a joy to visit. Some are world famous, like Barcelona's *La Boqueria*, or the market in Venice where fish are transported on boats. Pike Place Fish Market in Seattle is a real tourist attraction where the vendors have been throwing fish at each other for years. It's a great show so check out YouTube for videos. Whether it's the countless stalls piled high with glistening fresh fish on ice in *La Boqueria*, or Wieringen fish market in Den Oever (in the Dutch province of North Holland), fish markets are always busy and I could walk around them for hours.

In this chapter the focus is on herring, pike, langoustine and halibut. All are available at fish markets and, depending on the fishery, are sustainably caught. It's still advisable to be on your guard, however, as even responsibly farmed fish must be absolutely fresh. You should never trust a fishmonger who doesn't sell fresh fish. So what should you be looking for? Fish should never smell 'fishy' – fresh fish smells of the sea. It should be slippery and shiny and its skin should be covered in an even layer of slime. The eyes should be clear and the gills bright red inside. Choose a whole fish if possible as it's easier to check that it's fresh and the fishmonger can't craftily pass off haddock fillet as cod. You can always get the fishmonger to fillet the fish for you after you've bought it, and ask for the head and bones as you can use these to make stock. And always ask where the fish is from and how it was caught – the fishmonger should be able to answer both questions without any hesitation.

GRILLED LANGOUSTINES

CANAPÉ, STARTER, LUNCH — SERVES 4
PREPARATION **10 MINUTES** — COOKING **10 MINUTES**

Ferran Adrià was the celebrated chef at El Bulli, a three Michelin-starred restaurant in the small Spanish town of Roses, north of Barcelona, that has now closed but where in 1997 he began a culinary revolution with his molecular gastronomy. When asked who was his greatest inspiration, Adrià named Michel Guérard, Johan Cruijff and Rafa. French chef Guérard is one of the founders of nouvelle cuisine, Cruijff was one of the world's most famous footballers, but who's Rafa? I think Rafa Morales may well be my favourite chef. His restaurant, in Roses, is little more than a glorified canteen with just four or five tables. He cooks only fish – using olive oil or seawater – and, what's more, only the fish his brother has caught at sea that morning. He also matures his own anchovies in his cellar. Rafa cooks fish and nothing else so if you fancy a salad, you'll have to try across the road. But it's by far the best and freshest fish I've ever tasted, cooked simply under the grill (broiler), like these langoustines. In theory, you can always eat at Rafa's but three things could stand in the way: the weather could be too bad for his brother to go fishing, Barcelona's football team might be playing, or Rafa could feel uninspired. Even with a reservation, it's wise to call in the morning to check.

INGREDIENTS

1 litre/1¾ pints/4¼ cups court
  bouillon (see page 392)
16–20 raw langoustines
2 garlic cloves, finely chopped
handful of flat-leaf parsley,
  finely chopped
2 tbsp lemon juice
100 ml/3½ fl oz/generous
  ⅓ cup olive oil
2 tsp Pernod
1 tsp fleur de sel sea salt
salt and pepper

ALTERNATIVE SEAFOOD

frozen langoustines or crayfish

Preheat the grill (broiler).

Bring the court bouillon to the boil in a large pan, add the langoustines and cook for 3 minutes. Drain the langoustines from the pan and leave to cool.

Mix together the garlic, parsley, lemon juice and olive oil in a small bowl and season with salt and pepper.

Split the langoustines in half lengthwise, starting at the head. With the insides of the langoustines facing up, lay them side by side in a grill pan (broiler tray). Spoon the marinade over the langoustine flesh, reserving one quarter of it for serving. Drizzle over the Pernod.

Put the reserved marinade in a small saucepan over a low heat.

Grill the langoustines for 2–4 minutes until they are nicely browned on top.

Serve the langoustines in a dish with the reserved marinade spooned over and sprinkled with the fleur de sel.

ARROZ NEGRO

MAIN COURSE — SERVES 4
COOKING 45 MINUTES

The Catalan coastal village of Cadaqués is known to have been a favourite of leading artists such as Dalí, Miró and Picasso, and it's not difficult to see why. It lies at the end of a long road that runs through a nature park and although it has a pebble beach, the shore is one of the most beautiful anywhere. Cadaqués is my second home as it's where I get my inspiration, the place where I like to write my cookbooks and create new recipes. The beauty of this fishing village lies in its simplicity. In the main square, the Can Rafa restaurant is a real family affair where the father cooks what his son has caught at sea that morning, and the wine served is from their own vineyard. Perhaps it's the romance of the place, but the arroz negro at Can Rafa is the best I've ever tasted. Arroz negro is really a kind of paella that is tinted black with squid ink. It's not a dish I'd recommend you order at some beach café as its jet black colour means you can never be quite sure what's in it. However, at Can Rafa it is simple, always fresh, and always delicious. It's right here, sitting on a wooden chair in the square, that I want to grow old, with a nice glass of wine and a simple meal.

INGREDIENTS

2 onions, finely chopped
2 garlic cloves, finely chopped
1 red chilli (chile), deseeded and finely chopped
handful of flat-leaf parsley, finely chopped
1 x 400-g (14¹/₂-oz) can plum tomatoes, roughly chopped
400 g/14 oz cuttlefish, cleaned and cut into pieces
500 g/1 lb 2 oz/2 cups paella rice
200 ml/7 fl oz/scant 1 cup white wine
1.2 litres/2 pints/5 cups fish stock (see page 390)
50 g/2 oz squid ink
3 langoustines
4 tbsp aioli (see page 262)
olive oil for frying
salt and pepper

ALTERNATIVE SEAFOOD

frozen langoustines or crayfish

Heat 2 tablespoons of olive oil in a deep frying pan (skillet) or paella pan over a low heat and fry the onion, garlic and chilli (chile) until the onions are soft and translucent. Add the parsley and tomatoes and simmer for 20 minutes, stirring occasionally. Add the cuttlefish and cook for 2 minutes.

Add the rice and stir well until all the grains have become translucent. Deglaze with the white wine and cook until the liquid has been absorbed. Add the fish stock and squid ink and stir until the rice is uniformly black. Put the pan on a heat diffuser and cook the rice for 20–25 minutes over a low heat.

Cook the langoustines in a pan of boiling, salted water for 3–4 minutes (or in court bouillon, see page 392). Drain from the pan and keep warm. Check to see if the rice is cooked. If it is not quite tender, but all the liquid has been absorbed, cover the pan with foil and finish cooking it briefly in a hot oven.

Serve the rice topped with the langoustines and aioli on the side.

HERRING SALAD WITH WATERCRESS & HORSERADISH

STARTER, LUNCH — SERVES 4
PREPARATION 15 MINUTES — COOKING 15 MINUTES

Herring is a fantastic fish and there are many ways to eat it. In my home country in the Netherlands we eat them raw but they are fantastic smoked, pan-fried or marinated. In this simple salad we use marinated herring and the marinade itself to create a simple creamy dressing. A great dish for a summer lunch or sunset supper.

INGREDIENTS

400 g/14 oz baby new potatoes, peeled
300 g/10 oz sour herring fillets from a jar, liquid reserved
handful of fresh dill sprigs
4 tbsp crème fraîche (sour cream)
2 tsp creamed horseradish
2 drops of lemon juice
handful of watercress sprigs, coarse stalks removed, finely chopped
1 Granny Smith apple, cut into matchsticks
1 red onion, thinly sliced
salt and pepper

Boil the potatoes in a pan of lightly salted water for 10–15 minutes until just tender. Drain and leave to cool slightly. The potatoes will taste better if they are not served too cold and will absorb more flavours from the creamy dressing if still warm.

Cut the herring fillets into roughly 3-cm/1¼-inch pieces.

Pick over the sprigs of dill, discarding any tough stalks. Reserve a few for garnish and finely chop the rest.

Mix the crème fraîche (sour cream) with 1 tablespoon of the liquid from the herring jar and the horseradish. Season to taste with lemon juice, salt and pepper.

Halve the potatoes and add to the cream mixture. Stir well and add most of the chopped dill, chopped watercress, apple, red onion and herrings, reserving a little of everything to garnish the salad.

Serve the salad on a dish or plate, garnished with the reserved ingredients and dill sprigs. Season with freshly ground pepper.

KIPPERS WITH
MARSH SAMPHIRE BUTTER

BREAKFAST, LUNCH — SERVES 4
PREPARATION 10 MINUTES — COOKING 10 MINUTES

Kippers are hot smoked herring that are delicious served on toast. With the creaminess of the butter and saltiness of the samphire it is a hearty breakfast dish that is much-beloved by Brits. Good for after a night out with an egg on top – the perfect hangover cure.

INGREDIENTS

100 g/4 oz/8 tbsp butter, at room temperature
½ shallot, chopped
25 g/1 oz marsh samphire (sea asparagus/sea beans), finely chopped
1 tbsp lemon juice
4 kippers
4 slices of bread
pepper

Preheat the oven to 140°C/275°F/Gas Mark 1.

Melt 20 g/½ oz/¾ tablespoon of the butter in a frying pan (skillet) over a low heat. Add the shallot and marsh samphire (sea asparagus/sea beans) and fry for 30 seconds. Transfer to a bowl and leave to cool.

Mix the remaining butter with the marsh samphire and shallot mixture in the bowl and season with lemon juice and pepper. Taste and, if necessary, add a little salt but this may not be required as marsh samphire is already quite briny. Shape the butter into a roll and wrap in cling film (plastic wrap). Put the butter in the freezer to firm it up.

Heat the kippers in the oven for 4–5 minutes and, at the same time, toast the bread. Take the samphire butter from the freezer and remove the kippers from the oven.

Serve the kippers on the toast with a slice of the samphire butter on top.

CALAMARI COOKED ON A GRIDDLE

LUNCH, MAIN COURSE – SERVES 4
PREPARATION 5 MINUTES – COOKING 10 MINUTES

There is a fishery in the US that is looking for MSC-certification for its sustainable fishing practices using nets for catching squid. Octopus are found in all the seas and oceans of the world apart from the Black Sea. Cuttlefish, which live in coastal waters, are related to octopus, as are squid, which live in the open sea. Both look quite similar, having a conical-shaped body that ends in a point with a fin on either side. Two long tentacles and eight arms are attached to the head. Many people say they don't like squid because of its rubbery texture, but this is the result of incorrect cooking. The flesh of squid, like octopus, is much more delicate than that of ordinary fish, so the connective tissue is far tougher in order to add strength, with the result that squid must be cooked very quickly or stewed slowly. When cooked quickly, the flesh remains succulent and becomes almost crisp, but when cooked at 60°C/140°F or higher, the flesh shrinks and the squid curls as the connective tissue contracts. It is at this point that all the fluids are expelled from the flesh and so the squid becomes rubbery. If you leave it to simmer for another hour or so, the tough connective tissue breaks down and the result is a superbly tender squid. The long body is easy to slice into rings and fry in batter – the traditional calamari.

INGREDIENTS

500 g/1 lb 2oz squid, cleaned;
   heads and tentacles reserved
   (see page 401)
2 garlic cloves, finely chopped
handful of flat-leaf parsley,
   finely chopped
1 lemon, cut into wedges
extra vigin olive oil
salt and pepper

Pat the squid dry with kitchen paper (paper towels) and make shallow square-shaped incisions on one side of the body to prevent the flesh shrinking. Toss the squid with a dash of olive oil and season with salt and pepper. Heat a griddle pan or heavy frying pan (skillet) and sear the squid on both sides for 2–3 minutes until golden brown.

Reduce the heat to low and add 2 tablespoons of oil and the garlic and sauté the garlic until it is nice and crisp. Add the parsley, mix well and fry everything together briefly.

Transfer to a serving plate and accompany with lemon wedges to squeeze over.

GRILLED SWORDFISH WITH LENTILS & SALSA VERDE

MAIN — SERVES 4
PREPARATION **20 MINUTES** — COOKING **35 MINUTES**

Swordfish was one of my favourite fish species for many years but around 10 years ago it was revealed that swordfish was being overfished so I stopped consuming it. Now there are some responsible MSC-certified fisheries around the world I can begin to enjoy my favourite fish again. Like tuna it should be cooked quickly on a hot grill pan on both sides then gently over a cooler heat or in the oven to cook through to keep the flesh tender and not at all dry.

INGREDIENTS

4 x 150–170-g/5–6-oz
   swordfish steaks
vegetable oil, for frying
salt and pepper

LENTILS

180 g/6 oz/1 cup puy lentils
1 celery stalk
2 sprigs of thyme
5 sprigs of flat-leaf parsley
4 tbsp extra virgin olive oil
1 lemon
½ red onion, chopped
10 rocket (arugula) leaves
3 sprigs of basil, chopped

SALSA VERDE

2 tsp Dijon mustard
1 garlic clove
2 tbsp capers
5 sprigs of basil
5 sprigs of mint
10 sprigs of parsley
1 tbsp red wine vinegar
juice of ½ lemon
100 ml/3½ fl oz/⅔ cup extra
   virgin olive oil

Start by preparing the lentils. Put the puy lentils in a pan and cover with cold water. Add the celery, thyme, parsley stalks (save the leaves for later) and bring to a simmer. Don't add salt just yet. Simmer for 20–25 minutes until al dente and then drain. Remove and discard the celery, thyme and parsley.

Season the lentils while still warm with salt and pepper, olive oil, the zest of the whole lemon and the juice of half. When the lentils are completely cool add the red onion, rocket (arugula) and basil.

To make the salsa verde, add the mustard, garlic and capers to a food processor and blend to mix well. Add the basil, mint, parsley, red wine vinegar, lemon juice and olive oil. Blend well and season with salt and pepper to your own taste.

Set a grill pan over a medium-high heat. Season both sides of the swordfish steaks with salt and pepper and rub a little vegetable oil over both sides.

Grill the swordfish in the hot pan for 2–3 minutes on each side.

Serve the fish with the lentils and salsa verde drizzled on top.

OVEN-BAKED PLAICE WITH FENNEL & GARLIC

MAIN COURSE — SERVES 4
PREPARATION 15 MINUTES — COOKING 25 MINUTES

If you're cooking medium-size fish like mullet or plaice, it's always better to buy a whole fish. First – and most important – you can see whether it is fresh as, if it has its head on, the eyes should be clear and the gills bright red. If you're going to fillet the fish yourself, you can use the head and bones to make a well-flavoured stock. Cooking the whole fish on the bone will improve its flavour, as the skin stops the flesh drying out. The bones will also add to the flavour of the fish and there's one more secret – the cheeks. If you press below the eye with your thumbnail, a small round piece of fish will pop out and that's always the most succulent and tender part of a fish.

INGREDIENTS

4 x 300–400 g/10–14 oz plaice
   (or 2 larger fish weighing 600-
   800 g/1 lb 5 oz–
   1 lb 12 oz), rinsed
1–2 fennel bulbs, roughly
   chopped
2 onions, unpeeled and roughly
   sliced
1 lemon, sliced
zest of ½ orange, cut into strips
small bunch of thyme sprigs
1 garlic clove, finely chopped
3 garlic bulbs, cut in half across
   the centre
extra virgin olive oil
1 lemon, cut into wedges
salt and pepper

Preheat the oven to 180°C/350°F/Gas Mark 4.

Lightly grease 1 large (or several smaller) ovenproof dishes with olive oil.

Cut diagonal slashes in the flesh of the fish on both sides at 2 cm/ ¾ inch intervals using a sharp knife and lift into the ovenproof dish. Fill the cavity of the fish with some of the fennel and onions, the lemon slices, strips of orange zest and a few of the thyme sprigs. Drizzle over a little olive oil and season with salt and pepper.

Spoon a little olive oil into the slashes in the fish and push in the finely chopped garlic. Roughly chop a few sprigs of thyme and scatter over the fish. Sprinkle over salt and pepper and drizzle with a little more olive oil. Tuck the remaining fennel and onions, the halved garlic bulbs and a few more thyme sprigs around the fish.

Bake the fish in the oven, allowing 18–20 minutes for fish weighing up to 400 g/14 oz, and 2–4 minutes extra for every 100 g/4 oz of fish above that. Serve the plaice drizzled with a little extra olive oil and lemon segments to squeeze over.

SALT-CRUSTED PIKE PERCH

MAIN COURSE – SERVES 4
PREPARATION 15 MINUTES – COOKING 35 MINUTES

The great chefs of yesteryear – like Alain Senderens of Lucas Carton, who taught me to cook in Paris – never revealed their secrets. They would never present a recipe exactly the way they made it in the restaurant. But why all the secrecy? When Jamie Oliver arrived on our screens and his first books were published, we breathed a sigh of relief. Instead of acting mysteriously, he said, 'Look how easy it is, just do it.' He wants cooking to be fun and food to be tasty, but at the same time he encourages us to think about the provenance of the food we eat. Because of this he is a great example to me. When I was thinking about writing a new cookbook and making some videos a few years ago, a friend of mine suggested rather naively: you should do something with Jamie Oliver. This of course seemed like an unachievable dream. Shortly after launching my Instagram recipe videos with the 'shortest cooking programme in the world' I got a message from Jamie asking whether I wanted to make videos for his channel. A dream come true! A few months later we were recording in a studio, making fish baked in a salt crust just like the one on this page. Enjoy!

INGREDIENTS

1 whole pike perch weighing about 1.5 kg/3 lb 5 oz, or 2 smaller fish, cleaned and rinsed
handful of leaf coriander (cilantro)
1 lime, sliced
2 lemongrass stalks, roughly chopped
2.5 kg/5 lb 5 oz coarse sea salt
4 egg whites, lightly whisked with a fork

MISO SAUCE

3 tbsp white miso paste
1 tsp Dijon mustard
3 tbsp rice vinegar
2 tbsp mirin
4 tsp sugar
few drops of sesame oil
1 tsp soy sauce
1 cm/½ inch fresh root ginger, peeled and grated

ground coriander

Preheat the oven to 180°C/350°F/Gas Mark 4.

To prepare and cook the fish, pat the pike perch dry with kitchen paper (paper towels). Fill the cavity with half the coriander (cilantro), the lime slices and lemongrass.

Mix the coarse salt with the egg whites and a few drops of cold water. When the mixture sticks together, the consistency is right. Spread out half the salt mixture in an even layer in an ovenproof dish and lay the sea bass on top. Cover the fish with the rest of the salt, patting it down carefully to ensure the fish is completely covered. Bake the fish in the oven – if it weighs over 1 kg/2 lb 4 oz allow 30–35 minutes, for smaller pike perch allow 20–30 minutes, depending on size.

When the fish is almost ready, make the miso sauce. Put the miso paste, mustard, rice vinegar, mirin, sugar, sesame oil, soy sauce and a few drops of water in a small saucepan and whisk together over a medium-high heat until smooth. Stir in the ginger and heat the sauce without letting it boil.

Remove the fish from the oven and tap the back of a large knife on the salt crust until it breaks. Carefully remove the salt on top of the fish and slit open the skin lengthwise down the backbone with a knife. Fold the skin back to expose the flesh, which can then be lifted off the bone, taking care not to let the salt touch the flesh.

Serve the fish with the miso sauce and a pinch of ground coriander.

FRITTO MISTO

STARTER, LUNCH — SERVES 4
PREPARATION 40 MINUTES — COOKING 10 MINUTES

This book wouldn't be complete without me mentioning Hein Boersen, my favourite fisherman (pictured on page 295). Officially, he retired a long time ago, but he just can't seem to stop. He no longer sails as he used to in his large cutter; these days he goes out in a small sailing boat, *De Vrouwe Marie*. However, he still sails out of Den Oever harbour just as often – weather permitting. Hein Boersen fishes in the Wadden Sea, part of the North Sea between the West Frisian Islands and the northern Netherlands, for saltwater smelt. Freshwater smelt is found in IJsselmeer, a shallow lake in the central Netherlands, and you'll even find smelt swimming in the canals of Amsterdam. Smelt is a small fish, which you eat – head and all – freshly fried. It has a delicate flavour and a characteristic aroma of cucumber, which is why it's also known as 'cucumber fish'. MSC certified smelt is available from the Faroe Islands.

INGREDIENTS

BEER BATTER

160 g/5½ oz/generous 1 cup
   plain (all purpose) flour,
   sieved
1 egg
200 ml/7 fl oz beer/scant 1 cup
salt

FISH & VEGETABLES

1 lemon, sliced
2 small globe artichokes
2 red (bell) peppers
12 green asparagus spears
   (stalks)
8 squid, cleaned and thinly
   sliced into rings (see page 401)
200 g/7 oz smelt
16 medium raw prawns (shrimp),
   peeled and deveined (see
   page 395)
groundnut (peanut) oil for
   deep-frying

To make the batter, whisk the flour, egg and beer together with a pinch of salt until smooth. Chill in the refrigerator for at least 30 minutes, as the colder the batter, the lighter it will be when fried.

Grill (broil) the lemon slices on both sides in a ridged grill pan for 1–2 minutes. Cut the artichokes into eight, removing the 'hairs' and tough outer leaves with a small knife. Cut the (bell) peppers in half, deseed and slice the halves into thin strips. Trim 1 cm/½ inch off the base of each asparagus spear (stalk)

Heat oil for deep-frying to 180°C/350°F in a deep fat fryer or a deep heavy-based saucepan.

Dust the squid rings and prawns (shrimp) with flour and deep-fry for 3–4 minutes until golden and crisp. Deep-fry the smelt at the same time but do not dust them with flour. Drain onto a plate lined with kitchen paper (paper towels) and keep warm. Dust the vegetables with flour, dip in the batter until coated and deep-fry for 2 minutes until crisp. Drain on kitchen paper.

Sprinkle salt over the deep-fried seafood and vegetables and serve with the grilled lemon slices.

SWORDFISH CARPACCIO WITH LEMON CONFIT

STARTER, LUNCH — SERVES 4
PREPARATION 15 MINUTES

Carpaccio is a popular Italian starter made from wafer-thin slices of raw beef lightly drizzled with mayonnaise. Chef Arrigo Cipriani created the original dish in the 1960s at his celebrated Harry's Bar restaurant in Venice and he named it after the great Venetian Renaissance artist, Vittore Carpaccio, who was famed for his use of red and white in his paintings. Today, there are many variations of carpaccio, some served with pine kernels or shavings of truffle and Parmesan. Another increasingly popular variation is vegetable carpaccio made with vegetables such as thinly sliced mushrooms, tomato or beetroot (beet). And fish carpaccio, of course. Swordfish is perfect for serving in this way as it is quite a robust fish and is extremely tasty eaten raw.

INGREDIENTS

about 350 g/12 oz swordfish
    fillet, skin on
½ lemon confit (see page 391)
1 spring onion (scallion),
    trimmed and thinly sliced
4 tsp capers
a few chive stems, finely
    chopped
juice of ½ lemon
handful of mustard cress or
    fresh basil, finely chopped
extra virgin olive oil
salt and pepper

ALTERNATIVE FISH

salmon or grey mullet

Place the fish, skin side down, on a chopping board. Holding the fish steady with one hand and using a sharp filleting knife, cut the flesh into thin diagonal slices towards the tail.

Lay the slices on a large sheet of cling film (plastic wrap), cover loosely with another sheet and hit with the base of a long-handled pan or the flat side of a chopper to make them larger and thinner (see page 402).

Drizzle some olive oil over 4 serving plates to prevent the fish sticking to them. Divide the swordfish slices between the plates.

Cut away the flesh of the lemon confit from the white pith, cut the peel into thin strips and divide between the carpaccio. Scatter over the spring onion (scallion), capers and chives.

Drizzle 1 tablespoon of olive oil and a dash of lemon juice over each serving and garnish with the cress or basil. Season with salt and pepper and serve with country bread.

SAUCES & TECHNIQUES

Stock is an essential ingredient in many dishes and a number of the recipes in this book require stock to add flavour. Stock can also be used for poaching or steaming fish and it often forms the basis of a sauce.

The fish or shellfish stock you make yourself will undoubtedly taste the best. Stock is not difficult to make and it keeps well in the freezer. Here we explain how to make good-tasting stock, as well as stock for several hot and cold basic sauces. We also show you in easy to follow step-by-steps how to master the most common basic techniques, such as filleting different types of fish.

You can, of course, buy your fish ready-prepared from the fishmonger but it is much more satisfying to clean and fillet a whole fish yourself. It may look difficult, but these instructions, together with a little practice, will soon help you acquire the necessary skills. And the fish bones can be used to make another batch of delicious stock.

BASICS & SAUCES

FISH STOCK

Fish stock makes a good base for soups or sauces and can also be used for poaching and steaming fish.

INGREDIENTS FOR ABOUT 5 LITRES/
8¾ PINTS/10½ US PINTS

4 kg/9 lb fish bones and heads from white fish (e.g. sole, halibut, plaice, turbot, cod, haddock, sea bass)
25 g/1 oz/2 tbsp butter
3 onions, roughly chopped
2 leeks, trimmed, green parts removed, and roughly chopped
2 celery sticks, roughly chopped
2 carrots, roughly chopped
handful of flat-leaf parsley
100 ml/3½ fl oz/⅓ cup white wine
about 5 litres/8¾ pints/10½ US pints water
2 bay leaves
10 black peppercorns

Rinse the fish bones and heads thoroughly under cold, running water to wash away any blood still sticking to them. Roughly chop the bones and heads.

Add the butter to a large saucepan over a medium-high heat and when the butter has melted, add the onions, leeks, celery, carrots and parsley and cook, for 3–4 minutes until the vegetables have started to become translucent and have softened slightly. Add the fish bones and heads and fry for 2 minutes then pour in the wine and sufficient water to just cover the fish. Add the bay leaves and black peppercorns, turn up the heat. Bring the liquid to simmering point, around 90°C/195°F.

Use a skimmer or slotted spoon to remove any scum that forms on the surface. After 25 minutes, strain the liquid through a fine sieve or, even better, through a piece of muslin. The stock is now ready to use.

SHELLFISH STOCK

This stock can be used as a base for shellfish soups or risottos.

INGREDIENTS FOR ABOUT
3 LITRES/5¼ PINTS/6¼ US PINTS

3 tbsp groundnut (peanut) oil
4 kg/9 lb shellfish debris, e.g. heads, shells, tails
3 onions, roughly chopped
2 leeks, trimmed, green parts removed, and roughly chopped
2 celery sticks, roughly chopped
2 carrots, roughly chopped
1 head of fennel, thinly sliced
handful of flat-leaf parsley
2 tbsp tomato purée (paste)
3 tbsp Cognac
about 100 ml/3½ fl oz/generous ⅓ cup white wine
4 tsp Pernod
3 litres/5¼ pints/6¼ US pints water
2 bay leaves

Heat the oil in a large wide saucepan or deep frying pan (skillet), add the shellfish debris and fry for 5 minutes over a high heat. Add the onions, leeks, celery, carrots, fennel and parsley, stir over the heat for 1 minute and then add the tomato purée (paste).

Stir for 2 minutes and then deglaze the pan with the Cognac, white wine and Pernod. Pour in sufficient water to cover the shellfish debris and vegetables. Add the bay leaves and simmer the stock for 30 minutes, skimming off any scum that forms on the surface.

Strain through a fine sieve. The stock is now ready to use.

MAYONNAISE

INGREDIENTS FOR 250 ML/
8 ½ FL OZ/1 CUP

1 egg yolk
2 tsp Dijon mustard
½ tbsp white wine vinegar
a few drops of Worcestershire sauce
150 ml/5 fl oz/⅔ cup sunflower oil
½ tbsp lemon juice (optional)
salt and pepper

Make sure all the ingredients are at room temperature. Put the egg yolk in a bowl and whisk in the mustard, vinegar and Worcestershire sauce. Season with salt and pepper.

Whisking constantly, gradually drizzle in the oil a little at a time until it has all been added and the sauce is thick and creamy. Season to taste with lemon juice and more salt and pepper, if needed.

LEMON CONFIT

INGREDIENTS FOR 8 LEMON CONFIT

coarse sea salt
8 lemons

Put 2 tablespoons of sea salt in a preserving jar. Cut a cross in the top of each lemon, cutting two-thirds of the way down. Spoon 1 teaspoon of salt into the cuts in each lemon and pack them into the jar, pushing them down as firmly as possible. Fill the jar to the brim with sea salt, seal with an airtight lid and store in a cool dark place.

Leave for 3–4 weeks, after which time the lemons are ready to use. It is just the peel that is eaten.

MAYONNAISE-BASED SAUCES

There are several excellent and well-known sauces that go with fish, which are made by adding additional ingredients to mayonnaise.

REMOULADE SAUCE

Mayonnaise with finely chopped shallot, capers, gherkins, chives and parsley.

TARTARE SAUCE

Same as remoulade sauce, with the addition of a sieved or finely chopped hard-boiled egg.

COCKTAIL SAUCE

Mayonnaise with whipped cream, tomato ketchup, whisky (or Cognac) and cayenne pepper, to taste.

SHALLOT VINAIGRETTE

This goes well with oysters.

INGREDIENTS FOR 250 ML/
8 ½ FL OZ/1 CUP

red wine vinegar
1 shallot, finely chopped

Stir the vinegar and shallot together.

COURT BOUILLON

Court bouillon is perfect for cooking shellfish.

INGREDIENTS FOR ABOUT
4 LITRES/7 PINTS/8 ½ US PINTS

4 litres/7 pints/8½ US pints water
250 ml/8 fl oz/1 cup white wine
3 tbsp white wine vinegar
2 onions, roughly chopped
1 carrot, roughly chopped
1 leek, trimmed, green parts removed, and roughly chopped
handful of flat-leaf parsley
2 bay leaves
10 peppercorns
salt

Put all the ingredients in a large saucepan and bring to the boil over a high heat. Turn the heat down to medium and leave to simmer for 20–25 minutes.

Strain the bouillon through a fine sieve. It is now ready for use.

CLARIFIED BUTTER

Clarifying butter separates the milk solids and water from the butterfat, It prevents the butter burning too quickly so it is more suitable than ordinary butter for frying at a high temperature and for making beurre noisette (see page 365).

INGREDIENTS FOR 250 G/8 FL OZ/
1 CUP

300 g/10 oz butter

Melt the butter in a pan over a low heat, taking care not to let the butter brown.

Remove the pan from the heat and skim off the foam on the surface with a spoon.

Carefully pour the clear liquid fat into a bowl, leaving the milky residue behind in the pan. The fat in the bowl is the clarified butter.

SAUCE VIERGE

This is good served with fried, grilled or steamed fish.

INGREDIENTS FOR ABOUT 100 ML/
3 ½ FL OZ/GENEROUS ⅓ CUP

1 large ripe tomato
1 shallot, finely chopped
2 tbsp lemon juice
2 tbsp basil leaves, cut into thin strips
5 tbsp extra virgin olive oil
salt and pepper

Cut a cross into the base of the tomato. Put it in a pan of boiling water, leave for 10–15 seconds and then lift out with a slotted spoon. Cool under cold running water, strip off the tomato skin and leave until cold. Cut the tomato in half, scoop out the seeds and dice the flesh.

Heat 2 tablespoons of the olive oil in a pan and fry the shallot for 2 minutes until translucent. Add the remaining oil, the diced tomato and lemon juice. Season with salt and pepper and add the basil. Simmer for 1 minute over a low heat, remove from the heat and serve.

SALSA VERDE

Serve this excellent sauce cold with fried or grilled fish.

INGREDIENTS FOR ABOUT 200 ML/
7 FL OZ/ SCANT 1 CUP

2 garlic cloves
4 tbsp capers
2 tsp Dijon mustard
handful of mint leaves
handful of flat-leaf parsley
handful of basil leaves
juice of 1 lemon
2 tbsp red wine vinegar
100 ml/3½ fl oz/generous ⅓ cup extra virgin olive oil
salt and pepper

Put all the ingredients in a blender or food processor and whizz together until smooth. Season with salt and pepper.

BEURRE BLANC

This traditional butter sauce is good to serve with fried, poached or steamed fish.

INGREDIENTS FOR ABOUT 200 ML/ 7 FL OZ/SCANT 1 CUP

1 shallot, finely chopped
3 tbsp white wine vinegar
100 ml/3½ fl oz/generous ⅓ cup white wine
150 g/5 oz/10 tbsp cold butter, diced
salt and pepper

Put the shallot, vinegar and white wine in a small pan and bring to the boil. Boil until reduced by two-thirds.

Remove the pan from the heat and strain the mixture. Bring the liquid – we call it *castric* in Dutch – back to the boil, and immediately turn the heat down to low.

Whisk in the diced butter, one piece at a time, without letting the liquid boil again. Once all the butter has been incorporated and you have a smooth, creamy sauce, remove it from the heat and season with salt and pepper.

HOLLANDAISE SAUCE

Ideal as an accompaniment to fried or poached fish.

INGREDIENTS FOR ABOUT 200 ML/ 7 FL OZ/SCANT 1 CUP

4 egg yolks
4 tsp lemon juice
175 g/6 oz clarified butter (see page 392)
salt and pepper

Bring a pan of water to the boil. Lower the heat and stand a heatproof bowl on top of the pan without letting the bottom of the bowl touch the water – this is called a 'bain-marie'. The steam from the hot water in the pan will heat the bowl.

Add the egg yolks, 4 tablespoons of water and the lemon juice to the bowl and whisk together until the mixture is pale, thick and airy.

Whisk in the butter, a little at a time. When all the butter has been added and the sauce is thick enough, remove the bowl from the pan and season the sauce with salt and pepper.

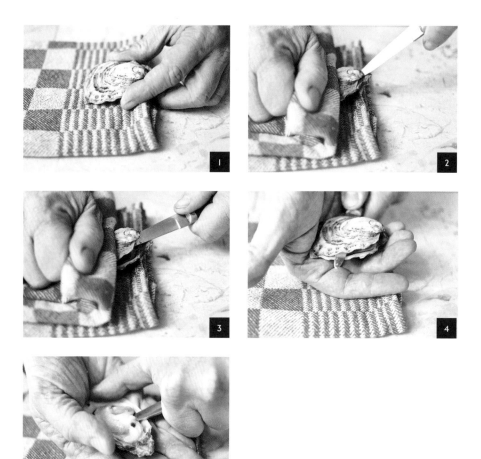

OPENING OYSTERS

STEP 1   Lay a folded tea towel (dish towel) on the kitchen worktop and place the oyster on the towel with the flat side of the shell uppermost.

STEP 2   Fold one side of the towel partly over the oyster with the hinge where the shells meet protruding. With an oyster knife in your other hand, work the tip into the hinge.

STEP 3   Wiggle the knife up and down to prise the two shells apart.

STEP 4   Put the oyster in the palm of your hand with the flat side up. Lift the upper half of the shell slightly with the knife and, moving slowly, work the knife under the upper shell to open the oyster.

STEP 5   Release the oyster meat by cutting it away from the lower shell. The oyster is now ready to eat or to use for your recipe.

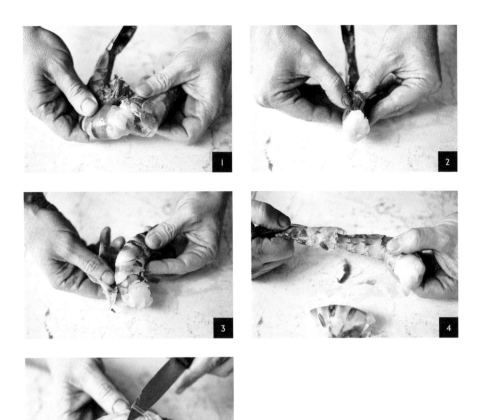

PEELING PRAWNS (SHRIMP)

Here we show you how to peel a large prawn (shrimp) but the technique is the same for peeling smaller prawns.

STEP 1 Twist the head of the prawn and carefully pull it away from the body.

STEP 2 Loosen the shell of the prawn from the underside.

STEP 3 Peel the shell away from the body as far as the tail.

STEP 4 When you reach the tail, hold the tip of it between your thumb and index finger and pull the prawn away from the shell.

STEP 5 Remove the intestinal tract by cutting a shallow incision down the back of the prawn and pulling out the dark thread with the tip of a small knife.

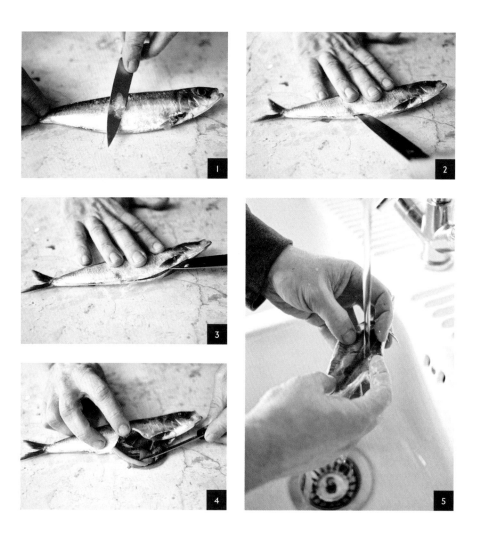

CLEANING SMALL ROUNDFISH

STEP 1 With one hand, hold the fish firmly by its tail and, with the other hand, run a small kitchen knife down the length of the fish from the tail towards the head to scrape off the scales.

STEP 2 Rest one hand lightly on the fish. Take a small kitchen knife in your other hand and cut open the belly of the fish, starting about 2 cm/½ inch from the tail.

STEP 3 Cut all the way up to the head.

STEP 4 Scrape the innards out of the belly cavity and discard.

STEP 5 Rinse the fish thoroughly inside and out under cold running water.

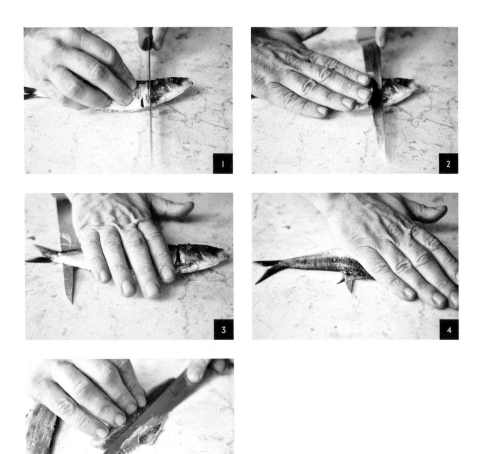

FILLETING SMALL ROUNDFISH

STEP 1 Put the fish flat on a board and, holding a kitchen knife vertically, cut through the flesh of the fish behind the head as far as the backbone.

STEP 2 Turn the blade from vertical to horizontal so it faces towards the tail and hold the fish down with the other hand by resting it on the flesh.

STEP 3 Slice the fillet away from the bone all the way from the head to the tail in one movement.

STEP 4 Turn the fish over and repeat on the other side.

STEP 5 Trim the edges of the fillets neatly.

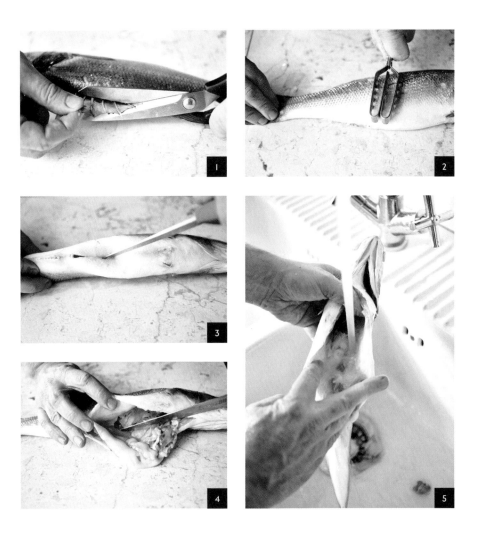

CLEANING LARGE ROUNDFISH

STEP 1   Take a pair of kitchen scissors and snip off all the fins from the fish.

STEP 2   Hold the fish by its tail and, using a fish scaler, scrape off the scales working from the tail towards the head. Alternatively, you can use the back of a kitchen knife, but be careful not to tear the skin.

STEP 3   With the tip of a filleting knife, make a shallow cut in the belly of the fish, starting at the small hole one third of the way up from the tail and working towards the head.

STEP 4   Scrape out the innards from the abdominal cavity with the knife or pull them out with your fingers.

STEP 5   Thoroughly rinse the fish inside and out under cold running water.

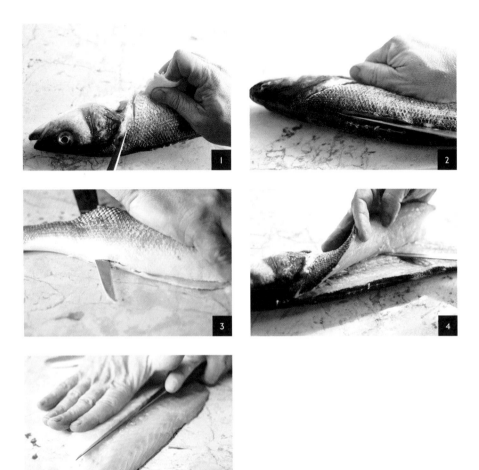

FILLETING LARGE ROUNDFISH

STEP 1   Slice open the belly of the fish. Run the knife down the back of the fish, starting at the head and cutting until you hit the backbone.

STEP 2   Hold the fish firmly by putting one hand in the abdominal cavity. With a filleting knife in your other hand, work the flesh away on one side starting at the head and cutting along the backbone, but not too deeply, only about 1 cm/½ inch into the flesh. Do this again, but cut more deeply into the flesh this time.

STEP 3   Slide the knife into the fish about one-third of the way up from the tail and cut the fillet away from the bone in one movement.

STEP 4   Finish cutting the fillet away from the bone at the head end.

Repeat this process to remove the fillet on the other side of the fish as well.

STEP 5   Trim the fillets and pull out any remaining tiny bones with tweezers.

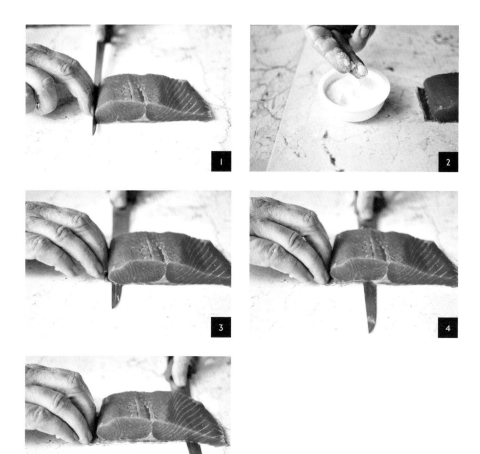

REMOVING THE SKIN
FROM A FISH

STEP 1 Put the fish fillet, skin side down, on a chopping board. Using a long-bladed, sharp knife, make a small cut down one side of the fillet between the skin and the flesh, large enough so you can grip the skin with your other hand.

STEP 2 Press down on the piece of loosened skin with your index and middle fingers – dipping your fingers first in water and salt to help you hold the skin more firmly.

STEP 3 Position the knife diagonally against the skin and cut with short horizontal movements between the flesh and the skin, keeping hold of the skin with your other hand.

STEPS 4 AND 5 Use short strokes to separate the flesh of the fish from the skin.

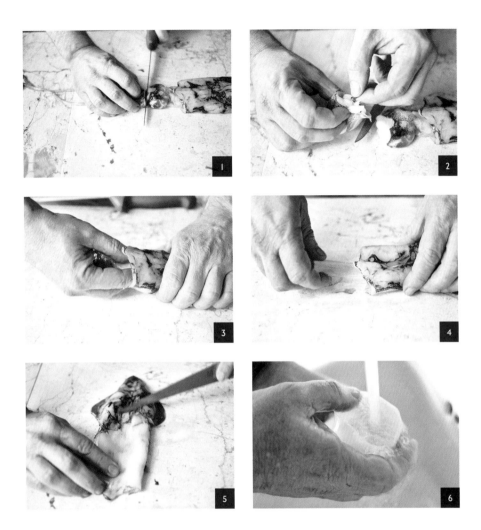

CLEANING SQUID

STEP 1 Cut the tentacles off the head, just below the eyes.

STEP 2 Remove the hard piece – the beak – from between the tentacles and discard.

STEP 3 Holding the squid in one hand, pull out all the innards with the other hand.

STEP 4 Remove and discard the long, plastic-like quill disc.

STEP 5 Pull the skin off downwards, starting at the broad end, carefully removing any pieces of skin that remain with a small knife. You could also use a small knife to scrape the skin away and clean the whole squid.

STEP 6 Rinse the squid lightly inside and out under cold running water.

SLICING CARPACCIO

STEP 1 Cut the fish into as thin slices as possible.

STEP 2 Place a slice of fish on a sheet of cling film (plastic wrap). The sheet should be about four times the size of the slice of fish.

STEP 3 Wrap the cling film over and around the slice.

STEP 4 Flatten the slice by beating it with a chopper (held horizontally) to make the slice thinner and larger. Repeat for each slice of fish.

STEP 5 Arrange the slices of fish on a plate, carefully pulling away the cling film (plastic wrap).

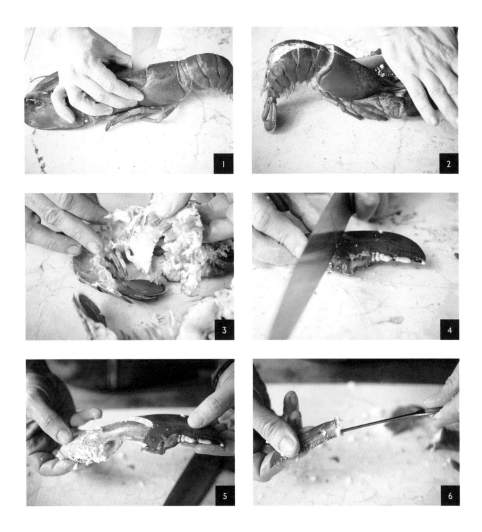

REMOVING THE MEAT FROM A COOKED LOBSTER

STEP 1 Plunge a large sharp knife into the back of the lobster and cut down the middle, first towards the tail and then through the head.

STEP 2 Turn the lobster over and cut down the middle on the other side to divide the lobster into two halves. Carefully remove the intestinal tract with your fingers or a small knife.

STEP 3 Put the two halves on a chopping board and remove the meat from the shell.

STEP 4 Break off the claws.

STEP 5 Pull out the meat from the smaller sections of the claws with your fingers. Break the shell of the larger sections of the claws by carefully cracking with the back of a heavy knife.

STEP 6 Remove the remaining meat from the claws using a pick.

THANKS EVERYONE

David Loftus! It's been my dream to work with you for so long – now it's happened and we've produced a wonderful book together. It was a great pleasure to travel with you and to be there when you took those amazing photographs – not to mention all those bottles of rosé we got through while we talked about the book, food and life. Many thanks!

Thank you lovely Inge Tichelaar. We've been great friends for years and now we've done a book together. And what a book! It was a massive leap in the dark, but I'm really so happy with the result and proud that you managed to pull it off. All those hours of talking, hours of cooking and so much laughter. You've made so many beautiful things. Love you!

Joël Broekaert. What an incredible guy! You're the fish expert in journalism, bar none. We've travelled to such beautiful places and what a joy it has been. Thank you for putting my feelings into words so well.

Thank you Arjan Weenink and Martijn Griffioen at Overamstel publishers. It's fantastic that you took on the challenge of making this mega project happen. It took guts and I feel so privileged that you put your faith in me – thank you. My thanks also to Marieke Dijkman for your inspiration, boundless energy and organization, all of which made this book possible. Thanks also to Marcus Turner, Ruth Visser and all the others at Overamstel Uitgevers.

Many thanks to Pavilion Books for giving us the opportunity to bring the book around the world. Thank you Katie Cowan for the trust and support – it's been lovely working together. Many thanks to Stephanie Milner for your fantastic work to the English edition of the book. Thank you Komal Patel for all your help with publicity. Thank you to Jackie Strachan and Jane Moseley for organizing the translation by Rosemary Mitchell-Schuitevoerder and Sam Hernan. And to Wendy Sweetser who edited the translated text.

Tijs Koelemeijer, what a stunning design you have made! We go way back now and I am so happy working with you and feel honoured that you took the chance to design this book. Thank you!

Ange Morris. Thanks for your dedication, support and care during the photo sessions in London. Julia Azzarello, thanks for your hard work, inspiration and effort at the food photography shoot in London.

Thank you Jamie Oliver for your amazing foreword and many thanks to Richard Herd and your team for the fantastic work and support at Jamie's Food Tube.

Thank you Lars Hamer for the great culinary support, to Suzanne Krom for editing and to Joke Jonkhoff for the corrections.

I want to thank Laura de Grave for editing the recipes and for organizing the trips we took. Thanks to Eline Ruigrok and Chantal Schram of Icelandair for making the flights to Reykjavik possible.

I'd like to thank Etihad Airways and, in particular, Olivia Heerenveen, Monique Irene de Voogd and Simon Kamsky for taking us so comfortably to the Maldives, India and Australia.

Special thanks to my buddy and amazing cameraman Tim van Niftrik. Great travelling with you!

Thanks also to Tony Tonnaer and K.O.I. (Kings of Indigo) for dressing me up using sustainable means.

At Fish Tales I'd also like to thank my partners Harm Jan van Dijk and Michiel Eliens. Thanks for your involvement and, above all, your patience. Thanks to Michael Verswijveren for cooking for the food photography shoots in Amsterdam and thanks to Nora van den Heuvel, Emiel Spelt, Laura van Hamburg, Rosa Zonneveld, Joost Swinkels, Gijs Stokvis and Danique Vogels for assisting. Thanks to Frank Barendse for your support, both business and personal.

Thank you to the Marine Stewardship Council (MSC) for your support for this book. Special thanks to Hans Nieuwenhuis and Sarah Bladen. Many thanks to Leslie Brazeau and Marin Hawk at MSC USA. Thank you to Meredith Epp at MSC Australia,. Let's make that change!

Thanks to Sarah Johnson, Rebecca Wilson of the Alaska Seafood Marketing Institute (ASMI), thanks to Niels Paauw and Ianna Niemeijer of Ka-Pow PR agency in the Netherlands, thanks to Ekkehard and Bianca Matthée of Elbfische PR agency in Germany.

Thank you everyone who helped us on our travels: John Burton, Abdul Razzaq, Ahmed Rasheed, Adnan Ali (Maldives), Vinod Malayilethu, Silvi Thomas and family, Dr Appukuttan (India), Svavar Þór Guðmundsson, Gunnar Ó Sigmarsson, Björgvin Þór Björgvinsson, Stéfan Vidarsson, Icelandairhotels (Iceland), Osborne Burke (Canada), Miren Garmendia, Sebastian Aranguren and Mila Oliveri (Spain), George Clark, Alan Dwan, David Pascoe (Cornwall, UK), Joop Pauwe, Freddy Klapwijk, Jan Kruijsse, Simon Schot, Martijn van der Sluijs, Hein Boersen (Netherlands), Dawda Saine, Ibrahima Niamadio (Gambia), Gary Bauer, Mitch, Roy and Shirley at Ponchartrain Blue Crab (Slidell, USA), Adam Watkins, Leah Watkins, Lenny Franklin and all fishermen at MG Kailis staff (Australia), the Chelsea Fishmonger (London, UK) and everyone else involved in these wonderful travels.

My lovely Bernadien, Bo, Juul and Ties! Thank you for your love, support, involvement, patience and inspiration! Love, love, love you!!!

RECIPE INDEX

INGREDIENTS INDEX

RESOURCES

All the recipes featured in this book can be found in video format online on my YouTube channel. Scan this code to go straight there to find a video that walks you through each one:

WEBSITES CONSULTED
www.fishbase.org
www.goedevis.nl
www.msc.org

FISHING FRIENDS
p.23 Skipper Hoessein
p.19 Ahmed Rasheed (Left)
p.56 Kerry Grace (Bottom left)
p.113 Margharita Thomas
p.151 Óli Sigmarsson
p.138 Aaron (Top right)
p.206 Alan Dwan
p.295 Hein Boersen

CREDITS

Concept and recipes: Bart van Olphen
Photography: All David Loftus except page 6 by
Ella Miller for Jamie Oliver Enterprises Limited
Text: Joël Broekaert
Design and illustrations: Tijs Koelemeijer
Styling: Inge Tichelaar
Styling assistant: Ange Morris
Culinary editing: Lars Hamer
Translation: JMS Books LLP, Rosemary
Mitchell-Schuitevoerder and Sam Hernan
Copy editor: Wendy Sweetser

With special thanks to Etihad Airways who supported the travel around the world to bring this book to life.
www.etihad.com

First published in the United Kingdom in 2017 by
Pavilion
43 Great Ormond Street
London
WC1N 3HZ

ISBN 978-1-91159-506-9

A CIP catalogue record for this book is available from the British Library.

10 9 8 7 6 5 4 3 2 1

Reproduction by Mission Productions, Hong Kong
Printed and bound by Dream Colour Ltd, China

This book can be ordered direct from the publisher at
www.pavilionbooks.com
www.fish-tales.com